Law for Professionals

The *Law for Professionals* book series contains publications in all fields of the law aimed at professionals and practitioners. The book series is dedicated to publish high quality books that provide in-depth insights into the workings and the practical functioning of the law, international organizations or regional legal frameworks.

The authors contributing to the book series are experienced legal professionals and practitioners whose expertise combines theory and practice.

Teresa Bravo • Kieran Bradley
Editors

Judicial Review in International Administrative Law

Springer

Editors
Teresa Bravo
United Nations Dispute Tribunal
Lisboa, Portugal

Kieran Bradley
IMF Administrative Tribunal
Luxembourg, Luxembourg

ISSN 2662-141X ISSN 2662-1428 (electronic)
Law for Professionals
ISBN 978-3-031-71839-7 ISBN 978-3-031-71840-3 (eBook)
https://doi.org/10.1007/978-3-031-71840-3

This Springer imprint is published by the registered company Springer Nature Switzerland AG
The registered company address is: Gewerbestrasse 11, 6330 Cham, Switzerland

Preface

International organisations are financed through contributions of member states and they pursue interests of public nature, being those of a humanitarian or financial scope. There is, undoubtedly, a public dimension in their mandates that justifies scrutiny and accountability from civil society.

Nonetheless, their internal functioning, as well as their managerial practises towards staff members and contractors is usually kept outside the public eye, unless a scandal occurs.

The underlying idea of this book was to render international organisations more visible, and transparent, and to bring in public opinion closer to institutions like the United Nations (and its different agencies) and multinational financial institutions.

Due to their jurisdictional immunity, these organisations have created their own internal justice systems which are insulated from national laws and jurisdictions and operate autonomously, within a restricted environment with exclusive rules and regulations. This is the context in which international administrative law has emerged and developed.

However, after serving for seven years as a full-time judge in the United Nations internal justice system, in Geneva, I have realised there was a gap in the (editorial) field of international administrative law and felt it was time to gather a group of professionals, willing to share their visions and experience in a book format.

Indeed, despite the existence of some (older) books and articles written on this topic, mostly by scholars, researchers and law professors, no updated literature which would convey practitioners' perspectives was readily accessible.

Judges and lawyers are sometimes reluctant to share their professional experience in a scholarly format and most of them are of the view that they should only communicate "through judgements" and "pleadings" rather than producing academic essays.

This book does not intend to fill any academic gaps, nor should the chapters included therein be seen as academic essays. Instead, it aims at contributing to a broader contemporary debate on specific issues international administrative tribunals face, from a practitioner's point of view.

Our target audience would be all curious readers and members of the public, with or without legal training, who are interested in knowing more about the functioning of those internal justice systems and the challenges they face. Staff members of international organisations and international civil servants may also feel inclined to read it to understand more about the functioning and the legal architecture of these internal justice mechanisms.

Consequently, the reader should not expect to find lengthy and over-conceptualised works in this book but rather an updated overview of the most recent jurisprudence produced by some international administrative tribunals and, particularly, the United Nations tribunals (UNDT and UNAT), the International Labour Organisation Administrative Tribunal (ILOAT) in the fields of sexual harassment and sexual exploitation, gathering of evidence, standards of proof in disciplinary procedures and internal investigations, as well as the role of staff associations.

All the contributors are experienced professionals in this field of law, working in the internal justice system of important international organisations or have had previous working experience in those organisations as judges, investigators, mediators or senior legal counsel. As such, their perspective comes directly from the field and reflects their professional daily practise.

The first chapter in this book specifically addresses legal standing before the United Nations Dispute Tribunal (UNDT) and the role of staff associations. The purpose of this chapter was to clarify why those tribunals cannot be seen as "internal labour courts" and explain the limits and scope of their judicial review powers, which are considered to be "too narrow" and their jurisprudence "detrimental" to staff members.

In this regard, it is also important to highlight the contribution of the Executive Secretary of the Administrative Tribunal of the Inter-American Development Bank Group, Giuliana Canè, who explains in detail the organisation and the work produced by that administrative tribunal and the challenges it faces.

On a more substantive dimension, Judge Peay (former judge of the Administrative Tribunal of the Organisation of American States) and Judge Donaldson Honeywell (half-time judge of the UNDT) offer the reader a diverse and comprehensive review of the most recent jurisprudence on standards of proof and legal issues emerging in cases of sexual exploitation and harassment.

Judge Bradley's chapter explores the origins of the standard of proof—"beyond reasonable doubt"—which has been adopted by the ILOAT in disciplinary cases, and highlights the challenges posed by this test, particularly in the area of disputes about harassment at the workplace.

This is, indeed, a hot topic not only for the UN agencies (which work in field missions under extremely difficult conditions and where these incidents appear to happen more frequently) but also for other international institutions where complaints of sexual harassment and abuse have been made against senior managers and peers by several staff members, mostly women.

In addition, the chapter written by Ruth Szabo, a former UN senior legal counsel and investigator, illustrates in a clear and detailed manner, the main trends in the ILOAT jurisprudence in cases of sexual harassment and provides the reader with a realistic picture of how IOs deal with those investigations as well as the main constraints they face.

One of the most difficult issues raised by complaints of sexual harassment, sexual exploitation and abuse is the necessity to reconcile victims' and subjects' due process rights in the context of internal investigations and disciplinary procedures. In many situations, victims are reluctant to testify and refuse to be cross-examined, whereas the tribunal does not have subpoena powers and therefore, cannot bring the witness to stand.

On the other hand, during investigations and disciplinary proceedings, subjects are frequently placed on special leave with or without pay (SLWP/SLWOP) for several months or years, before a final determination is made, which places a heavy burden on someone who is presumed innocent.

The chapters contained in the book address these topics and render them more visible, while paving the way for further development in this field of law.

Nonetheless, the authors have only made use of publicly available information and did not disclose any names, nor the identities of the people involved in the cases that are mentioned in their contributions, to protect their privacy rights and private life details.

Also, the chapters contained in the book do not represent any official view of the organisations which are cited therein but express only the personal opinions of its authors and do not prejudice the position the author may subsequently adopt in her or his professional capacity.

All the involved in this project expect the book to be useful to all those readers who want to learn more about the work performed by international administrative tribunals and their judges, and hopefully, it will contribute to a more open approach and debate in this exciting field of law.

Lisbon, Portugal
12 August 2024

Teresa Bravo

Contents

Highlights of the Doctrine of Acquired Rights and the Jurisprudence of International Administrative Tribunals 1
Teresa Bravo

Institutional Setting of Administrative Tribunals: The Case of the Inter-American Development Bank Administrative Tribunal (IDBAT), with References to Its Peers 15
Giuliana Canè

Legal Standing Before (International) Administrative Tribunals and the Role of Staff Associations 37
Teresa Bravo

Harassment Investigations in International Organizations: Rights of Claimants under the Jurisprudence of the International Labour Organization Administrative Tribunal (ILOAT) 53
Ruth Szabó

The United Nations Jurisprudence on Pre-disciplinary Cases Involving Sexual Exploitation and Abuse 75
Eleanor Donaldson-Honeywell

Divergent Standards of Proof Currently Applied by International Administrative Tribunals in Serious Misconduct Cases: An Evolving Snapshot 87
T. Michael Peay

Reasonable Doubt About Proof "Beyond Reasonable Doubt" in International Administrative Law 109
Kieran Bradley

Highlights of the Doctrine of Acquired Rights and the Jurisprudence of International Administrative Tribunals

Teresa Bravo

Contents

1 Introduction 1
2 (Re) Conceptualising Acquired Rights 2
3 The Jurisprudence of ILOAT and the World Bank Administrative Tribunal 3
3.1 The *Ayoub* test 4
3.2 *De Merode* Judgement of the WBAT 5
4 UNDT's Case Law on "*Acquired Rights*" 8
4.1 A Divergent View from the United Nations Appeals Tribunal 9
5 Conclusion 13
Jurisprudence 13
References 14

1 Introduction

International organisations enjoy jurisdictional immunity from member states, an essential instrument of their institutional autonomy, addressed at avoiding political interference in the execution of their mandates. These organisations have created internal justice systems which are totally distinct and independent from national jurisdictions since the applicable rules, procedures and statutes are those approved by internal legislative bodies.

Teresa Bravo, Judge and former President of the UNDT, currently Judge at the IADBAT and Asian Development Bank Administrative Tribunal

T. Bravo (✉)
United Nations Dispute Tribunal, Lisbon, Portugal

T. Bravo, K. Bradley (eds.), *Judicial Review in International Administrative Law*, Law for Professionals, https://doi.org/10.1007/978-3-031-71840-3_1

Consequently, these systems have their own internal tribunals and appeal boards, which produce their own set of jurisprudence. Based on its case law, a specific body of international legal principles has emerged.

One of the most significant principles that resulted from international administrative tribunals' case law is the protection of *acquired rights*. The scope and limits of its application have mainly been defined by the jurisprudence of ILOAT which has expanded to, and was assimilated by the case law of international financial institutions through "cross-fertilisation."

Cross-fertilisation (being a hermeneutical tool) has allowed different tribunals to import, adapt and apply similar legal solutions in different institutional contexts, while contributing to a certain level of convergence in this field of law.

Within the next pages, an overview of the most recent jurisprudence that has applied the principle of acquired rights will be provided and compared with previous judgements.

2 (Re) Conceptualising Acquired Rights

The concept of acquired rights in international administrative law has its roots in the jurisprudence of ILOAT (*Plissard*, Judgement No. 12 (1954), *Settino* Judgement No. 426 (1980), and more recently, in *Ayoub, Lindsey et al.* Judgement No. 3876 (2017).

Acquired rights refer to the set of rights which constitute a fundamental term of the employment relationship between the International Organisation, hereinafter IO and the staff member, which are expected to survive any amendments in the staff rules.

This concept is broader than the principle of non-retroactivity as it concerns not only the past but also the future (no future legislative changes can affect essential terms of a contract) and includes those rights that derive not only from contractual provisions but also from statutory provisions concerning the functioning of the international organisation.[1]

According to Rishi Gulati: *"There has been a general consensus that the acquired rights doctrine protects a staff member's essential terms of employment both retrospectively and prospectively. However, in its recent jurisprudence, the United Nations Appeals Tribunal or the UNAT has rendered the acquired rights doctrine with little work to do by reducing it to the principle of non-retroactivity. As a result, the consensus as to the doctrine's core meaning is now undermined. International civil servants having access to the ILOAT are much better protected from unilateral adverse amendments to their conditions of employment when compared to those international public officials whose organisations have subscribed to the jurisdiction of the UNAT. This is an unwelcome development for the content of*

[1] I would posit that this concept is substantive whereas non-retroactivity is a procedural principle that refers to the applicability of a given rule or regulation *ratione temporis*.

substantive protections is now more dependent on the tribunal approach, as opposed to a coherent development of the law."[2]

These latest developments in the jurisprudence of "acquired rights" justify, from our point of view, some reflection on how it has developed and in which direction are international administrative tribunals moving now.

Redefining the scope and boundaries of the principle of acquired rights has a huge impact on the employment status of international civil servants as it may either constitute a barrier or open a big door to future amendments of their benefits and entitlements that may impair the fragile balance of employment relationships in international organisations.

3 The Jurisprudence of ILOAT and the World Bank Administrative Tribunal

The *Ayoub* Case

Ayoub case refers to changes in the pension scheme of ILO staff which belongs to the "common system" of the United Nations. ILO staff members had, for 40 years, a pension scheme known as the United Nations Joint Staff Pension Fund ("the Fund"). A Joint Staff Pension Fund Board ("the Board"), set up by the General Assembly of the United Nations ("the Assembly"), runs the Fund and applies Fund Regulations.[3]

According to the judgement, the amount of pension depended on three things: the length of service of the staff member, the percentage of his remuneration that he/she is to get for each year of service and the third is "pensionable remuneration," which depends on each staff member's grade and his step within the grade which governs the amount of his pension contributions.

An actuarial evaluation of the Fund made on 31 December 1980 revealed a serious decline in its finances, the Board made proposals for savings which meant lower benefits, and the Assembly approved the proposals in Resolution 37/131 of 17 December 1982. To make further savings the Assembly decided in Resolution 39/246 of 10 December 1984 to adjust pensionable remuneration.

It approved a new scale of pensionable remuneration on 1 January 1985 and correspondingly amended Article 54(b) of the Fund Regulations to read:

> In the case of participants in the Professional and higher categories, the pensionable remuneration effective 1 January 1985 shall be as appears in the appendix to these Regulations.

---

[2] See, Gulati (2021), p. 82.

[3] See, Ayoub, Judgement No. 832 (2017), available online at https://webapps.ilo.org/dyn/triblex/triblexmain.fullText?p_lang=en&p_judgment_no=832&p_language_code=EN, accessed on 09 August 2024.

According to the new scale, which determined pensionable remuneration for each grade and step in the professional and higher categories, pensionable remuneration went up for grades P.1 and P.2 but fell for P.3 and above.

In the case presented before the ILOAT, the complainants were professional category staff of the International Labour Office. Their pay slips for April 1985 took account of the two circulars and they found that the new scale meant a reduction in their pension contributions and so also in the amount of their future pensions. They appealed to the director general who rejected their claims.

Despite confirming the legality of the contested decision (based on the financial constraints the organisation faced), the ILOAT's judgement is relevant due to the legal test it implemented, which helped to clarify the scope and limits of the doctrine of acquired rights.

3.1 The *Ayoub* test

ILOAT acknowledged in *Ayoub* that the doctrine of acquired right "cover[s] not just terms of appointment that were in effect at recruitment but also terms that were brought in later and were calculated to induce the staff member to stay on."

The test for determining whether a modification to a term or condition of service violates an acquired right, as it derives from the jurisprudence of international administrative tribunals, including the leading cases *De Merode et al.*[4] of the World Bank Administrative Tribunal (WBAT) and *Ayoub* from the ILOAT, may be summarised as follows.

1. First, the Tribunal must determine if the modification to the rules alters a term of employment that is "fundamental and essential in the balance of rights and duties of the staff member"; a change to a fundamental and essential term of appointment would violate staff members' acquired rights, irrespective of the reason for the change or the actual impact on the concerned staff members.
2. Therefore, the Tribunal must look at the terms of appointment contained in the letter of appointment and evaluate its nature;
3. If the altered term of appointment is found to be less fundamental and essential, the Tribunal must then examine, inter alia, the reasons for the change and its consequences for the staff members;

In ILOAT's own words: "By the lights of the Tribunal's case law and that of the World Bank Administrative Tribunal the pension scheme and the scale of pensionable remuneration are essential terms of an official's appointment, and he has an

[4] See, *De Merode et al.*, Decision N.1, held on 5 June 1981, available at: https://tribunal.worldbank.org/sites/default/files/Judgments%20and%20Orders/de%20Merode%2C%20Lamson%20Scribner%2C%20Jr.%2C%20Reese%2C%20Reisman%20Toof%2C%20Ruberl%2C%20Shapiro%20v.%20The%20World%20Bank.pdf, accessed on 09 August 2024.

acquired right in the matter. What must be safeguarded is terms of appointment not just as at the time of recruitment but also as revised from time to time. It is wrong to say that officials not on the brink of retirement have no interest in having the old and more favourable scale still apply to them. At the least they should be given an option."

For the ILOAT, the doctrine of acquired rights looks both at the past and the future, whereas the rule of non-retroactivity is only focused on the past:

> Stated in that way the doctrine is broader than the rule against retroactivity. Whereas the doctrine looks at the future as well as to the past, the rule merely forbids altering what already belongs to the past.

This judgement represented an evolution in relation to previous judgements of the same tribunal. In fact, as explained by Eva Gröninger-Voss,[5] three different stages can be identified in the evolution of the ILOAT's jurisprudence.

An early stage, in which the tribunal only considered acquired rights those resulting from contractual provisions (see, *Sheriff,* ILOAT No. 29), an intermediate step when the tribunal in Lindsey, ILOAT N. 61, recognised that acquired rights are not restricted to contractual provisions but can also derive from statutory provisions, if considered essential/fundamental and finally, the latest jurisprudence incorporated in *Ayoub*.

The essential/fundamental nature is established with a three-pronged test relating to the nature of the provision, the reason for the impugned change and its consequences.

3.2 *De Merode* Judgement of the WBAT

In *De Merode* judgement, the World Bank Administrative Tribunal has also addressed a similar legal issue, related to the principle of acquired rights. The Tribunal was requested to decide whether the implementation of the decisions adopted on 25 May 1979 by the Executive Directors of the Bank regarding tax reimbursement and salary adjustment (to inflation and cost of living) amounted to non-observance, by the Bank, of the Applicant's contracts of employment or terms of appointment.

Therefore, two main questions were at stake:

1. Does the World Bank have the power—and, if so, within what limits—to unilaterally change the conditions of employment of its staff?
2. May Bank personnel invoke the concept of acquired rights to prevent the application of changes unilaterally introduced by the Bank?

[5] See, Gröninger-Voss et al. (2017), pp. 109–128

First, the Tribunal recognised that the basic instrument on which the applicant's rights were based was their contract with the Bank. However, this was only one of many other elements "(. . .) which collectively establish the ensemble of conditions of employment operative between the Bank and its staff members."

The Tribunal has also recognised the Bank's inherent power to change the "(. . .) general and impersonal rules establishing the rights and duties of the staff. It is a well-established legal principle that the power to make rules implies in principle the right to amend them."

Nonetheless, the judges signalled that this power is not unfettered and there are limits to the Banks' exercise of administrative discretion:

> 42. (. . .) Certain elements are fundamental and essential in the balance of rights and duties of the staff member; they are not open to any change without the consent of the staff member affected. Others are less fundamental and less essential in this balance; they may be unilaterally changed by the Bank in the exercise of its power, subject to the limits and conditions (. . .).

The criteria used in *De Merode* judgement as limiting the unilateral power of the Bank to introduce changes to essential elements of the employment relationship, were the following:

1. Prohibition of a retroactive effect, as the Bank cannot deprive staff members of accrued rights for services already rendered;
2. Changes must be reasonably related to the objective they intend to achieve;
3. Changes must be made in good faith while taking into consideration the organisation's duty of care and causing minimal harm.

While affirming its own jurisdictional powers to review such decisions, the Tribunal was also careful in the sense that it considered it could not replace the decision-maker:

> 86. It is not for the Tribunal to substitute its judgment for that of the Bank in choosing the average deduction system, rather than some other system, to replace the previous system.

Consequently, in *De Merode* the WBAT concluded that the contested decisions were fully in accordance with the obligations of the Bank, and that it had not failed to observe the contracts of employment or terms of appointment of the Applicants.

In the United Nations system, the jurisprudence of the first instance tribunal—the UNDT—was aligned with ILOAT's case law and considered that acquired rights meant protection of essential terms of appointment both of statutory and contractual nature, for services already rendered as well as for the future.

However, as mentioned above, this was not the view of the appeals tribunal—UNAT which in 2018 quashed the first instance judgement (and the commonly accepted definition of acquired rights) and restricted its definition and scope to the principle of non-retroactivity, as will be explained below.

UNAT's jurisprudence represented a rupture with the previous jurisprudence of ILOAT and created a dangerous precedent in relation to the protection of staff members' rights leading to a manifestly unreasonable situation in the UN system, i.e. staff members placed in similar professional situations are treated differently.

In its Judgement No. 4134 (2018) ILOAT diverged from UNAT in relation to the ICSC's competence to review the compensation package of international civil servants and declared it illegal, while UNAT has confirmed the lawfulness of ICSCs' mandate allowing the implementation of the newly reviewed compensation package to all staff members falling under its jurisdiction.

In its judgement, ILOAT clearly assumed the risk of jurisprudential divergence with UNAT and opted to maintain its judicial independence, preserving its own views on the same legal issue:

> 29. In its judgments the Tribunal has recognised and accepted the existence of the United Nations common system and respected its objectives. However, the existence of the United Nations common system and a desire to maintain its integrity should not, in itself, compromise the Tribunal's adjudication of individual disputes in any particular case or series of cases involving the application of its principles.
>
> (...) The Tribunal has to recognise that an organization's legal obligations arising from the operation of the common system could have legal ramifications for an organization that inform or even determine the resolution of any particular dispute. However, notwithstanding these matters, the Tribunal must uphold a plea from a staff member or members if it is established that the organization has acted unlawfully.

The consequence was that international civil servants working in the UN common system or funds and programmes were affected by the implementation of the (new) compensation package whereas, those working for UN specialised agencies (under ILOAT's jurisdiction) were not affected, as the Tribunal confirmed the unlawfulness of its implementation.

Three years later, in Judgement 2021-UNAT-1108, the Appeals Tribunal acknowledged this jurisprudential divergence with ILOAT as follows:

> 73. There is one last aspect of this litigation upon which we comment briefly. We are aware that we have reached a decision which is apparently at odds with an earlier decision on the same questions reached by the International Labour Organisation's Administrative Tribunal (ILOAT). We will not comment on the ILOAT's judgment because it was reached on different grounds to those on which we have decided these appeals. We do note, nevertheless, that the fundamental structures under which each of the United Nations and International Labour Organisation judicial bodies operate differ considerably. The ILOAT, which was established well before the United Nations, is not part of the United Nations Administration of Justice system; its judges are not elected by the General Assembly; and this Appeals Tribunal is bound by United Nations General Assembly resolutions, some of which were cited in this Judgment, and particularly as they specifically refer to both the United Nations Dispute and Appeals Tribunals, but not the ILOAT.

According to UNAT, General Assembly (GA) resolutions, together with the Statute of the Appeals Tribunal, limit the scope of its judicial review: *"the remedy for the situation lies not in ignoring current statutory and legislative imperatives, but rather in the ability of the governing bodies of the two Organisations to effect change if they consider this is warranted."*

In the next chapter, we look closer at the reasoning of both UNDT and UNAT in relation to "acquired rights."

4 UNDT's Case Law on *"Acquired Rights"*

In 2017, the UNDT[6] in Geneva adjudicated a case in which the Applicants challenged the decisions "to reduce [their] contracted salary and the manner of the implementation of [a] Unified Salary Scale" effective 1 January 2017.[7]

Factual Background

Before the introduction of a Unified Salary Scale on 1 January 2017, staff members in the professional and higher categories were paid their net salary at either a single or a dependency rate, depending on their family status. They were also entitled to dependency allowances, depending on their family status, defined in ST/AI/2011/5 (Dependency status and dependency benefits).

In 2012, at its seventy-fifth session, the International Civil Service Commission ("ICSC") decided to initiate a comprehensive review of the compensation package for common system staff members, including the salary scale for staff members in the professional and higher categories, "to ensure that the pay and benefits provided to staff continued to be fit for purpose."

In its 2015 Report, the ICSC made its recommendation for the introduction of one net salary scale for all staff members in the professional and higher categories without regard to family status. Support provided for dependent family members would be separated from salary. The ICSC also recommended some changes to the eligibility criteria for this support. Amongst others, staff members with a non-dependent spouse at the time and in receipt of a salary at the dependency rate by virtue of a first dependent child would instead receive the child allowance for said child. Acknowledging that "[s]ome of those staff members would therefore experience significant reductions in salary under the proposed system," the ICSC proposed the introduction of a transitional allowance.

From a legal point of view, the UNDT had to decide whether the contested decisions infringed on applicants' contractual or acquired rights.

The Tribunal departed from Staff Regulation 12.1[8] to build its reasoning and considered said provision as a limitation to the legislative power of the organisation.

[6]See UNDT/GVA/2017/097, available online at https://www.un.org/internaljustice/oaj/en/judgment/undt2017097, accessed on 23 July 2024.

[7]The author was, by the time, a full-time judge in the UNDT and one of the panel members involved in the adjudication of this case at first instance level.

[8]"[t]he present Regulations may be supplemented or amended by the General Assembly, without prejudice to the acquired rights of staff members."

The Tribunal went even further and considered that "(...) pursuant to art. 101 of the UN Charter and staff regulation 12.1, the contracts between the Organization and the Applicants are composed of the terms explicitly set out in the letters of appointment and are also governed by the internal laws of the Organization, which the latter has the power to unilaterally modify, subject to the Applicants' acquired rights."

From the UNDT's perspective, in accepting their letter of appointment, staff members agree that their conditions of service may be subject to unilateral change by the organisation but only insofar as they do not touch upon their acquired rights.

The UNDT has also construed its reasoning based on the assertion that "protection of acquired rights" is a general principle of law and it is incumbent on an international organisation to respect its staff members' acquired rights, as acknowledged by the ILOAT in *Ayoub* (Judgement No. 832 (1987)), and even the former UNAT's jurisprudence, as it results from Judgement No. 273, *Mortished* (1981) and the separate opinion of Judge Stern in the former United Nations Administrative Tribunal Judgement No. 1253, *Ittah* (2005).

The UNDT recognised the "quasi constitutional nature of Staff Regulation 12.1" while stating that by its nature and content, Staff Regulation 12.1 and the acquired rights guaranteed therein take precedence over other staff regulations and rules governing the staff members' conditions of employment. From the Tribunals' point of view, the recognition of staff members' acquired rights would have no value and Staff Regulation 12.1 would be deprived of its meaning if the organisation was allowed to infringe on them by the mere adoption of conflicting staff regulations.

It is also noteworthy that, for the Tribunal, the terms and conditions of employment explicitly set out in the staff members' letters of appointment were considered as "acquired rights" by the former United Nations Administrative Tribunal (Judgement No. 19, *Kaplan* (1953)) and the ILOAT (Judgement No. 29, *Sheriff* (1957)).

Based on these premises, the UNDT considered the contested decision unlawful and ordered its rescission.

4.1 A Divergent View from the United Nations Appeals Tribunal

In 2018, Respondent appealed the UNDT's decision and, in its Judgement 2018-UNAT-840, the Appeals Tribunal reversed the findings and decision of the first instance, while narrowing the scope of "acquired rights" in a manner that contradicted the traditional doctrine.

The Appeals Tribunal started by denying that Staff Regulation 12.1 had a quasi-constitutional value against which other instruments should be reviewed on grounds of legality. It stated that the General Assembly's Resolution 13 (I) of 1946 and Staff Regulation 12.1 enjoy the same status in the normative hierarchy as all other General Assembly resolutions.

According to UNAT, the UNDT committed an error of law and considered that those provisions (Staff Regulation 12.1 and GA Resolution A/RES70/244, dated

23 December 2015[9]) must be construed in a way that they are capable of co-existing. From the appeals tribunal perspective, statutory instruments must be read together and the later one may be construed as repealing the provisions of the earlier one but only where that intention is explicit, or alteration is a necessary inference from the terms of the later statutory instrument.

For UNAT, this principle is captured in the *rule lex posterior priori derogat*—should there be an irreconcilable conflict between two enactments, the later enactment will take precedence over the earlier enactment and be held to have impliedly repealed the earlier enactment to the extent of the inconsistency.

UNAT considered that there was no doctrinal basis for the UNDT's finding that revocation or amendment of the earlier provision is required to be explicit or express and, if the provisions of Resolution A/RES/70/244 are irreconcilably inconsistent with the provisions of Resolution 13(I) of 1946, it is the later resolution which will take precedence. As such, any normative conflict would have to be decided in favour of the later resolution.

UNAT denied, therefore, the existence of a normative conflict or an irreconcilable inconsistency between Resolution 13(I) of 1946 and Resolution A/RES/ 70/244 and reinterpreted the term "acquired rights" in Staff Regulation 12.1 in a newly restrictive way.

The Appeal Tribunal took the view that the term "acquired rights" and the protection afforded by Staff Regulation 12.1 were inherently vague and ambiguous.

Thus, the aim of the intended protection would be merely to ensure that staff members' terms and conditions may not be amended in a way that would deprive them of a benefit once the legal requirements for claiming the benefit have been fulfilled, i.e. once the right to counter-performance (the salary or benefit) has vested or been acquired through services already rendered, Resolution A/RES/70/244 not retrospectively take away any vested right to receive a benefit for services already rendered.

According to UNAT, an "acquired right" should be purposively interpreted to mean a vested right and employees only acquire a vested right to their salary for services already rendered:

> Promises to pay prospective benefits, including future salaries, may constitute contractual promises, but they are not acquired rights until such time as the quid pro quo for the promise has been performed or earned. Moreover, the fact that increases have been granted in the past, does not create an acquired right to future increases or pose a legal bar to a reduction in salary.

According to UNAT's judgement, the protection of acquired rights goes no further than guaranteeing that no amendment to the staff regulations may affect the benefits

[9]This resolution approved, in its chapter III, para 1, the common system compensation package and is available online at: https://documents.un.org/doc/undoc/gen/n15/458/91/pdf/n1545891.pdf?token=y4YwMhw3qnxMbKCkra&fe=true, accessed 23 July 2024.

that have accrued to, or have been earned by, a staff member for services rendered before the entry into force of the amendment—prohibition of retroactivity.

While balancing acquired rights vis-a-vis the interests of the organisation, UNAT made a clear choice in favour of the organisation and justified it, as follows:

> It is in the public interest that public authorities retain the freedom to exercise their discretionary or legislative powers. It can never be in the international public interest to contractually fetter the General Assembly in the exercise of its powers to make policy for the Organization. A body such as the General Assembly cannot be compelled to uphold a promise not to exercise its regulatory powers so as not to interfere with its contractual arrangements.

For the Appeals Tribunal, in the context of the United Nations system, salary entitlements of staff members are statutory in nature and may be unilaterally amended by the General Assembly. Staff members do not have a right, acquired or otherwise, to the continued application of the Staff Regulations and Rules—concerning the system of computation of their salaries—in force at the time they accepted employment for the entirety of their service.

Therefore, the Appeals Tribunal chose to perform a dynamic and narrower interpretation of acquired rights, to open the door for (future) changes in salaries and entitlements of staff:

> 104. It will be useful to begin with a general clarification regarding contractual versus statutory elements of the employment relation. A contractual relationship refers to the relationship between the staff member and the international organisation as evidenced in a contract, i.e., a bilateral act. The statutory relationship, on the other hand, is based on status, i.e., refers to the appointment of civil servants by acts of authority, which forms a relation in accordance with statutorily defined terms and conditions. An individual who agrees to enter the public service gives full consent to these terms and conditions, in other words, joins by adherence.

This jurisprudence is problematic for several reasons.

From my point of view, the intangibility of remuneration / salary is a widely and commonly accepted international labour law principle. Similarly, one can argue that acquired rights and intangibility of remuneration are *ius cogens* (as they do not depend on the existence of a written norm).

On the other hand, acquired rights go far beyond the principle of non-retroactivity because it does not relate to the temporal scope of application of a certain legal framework, it relates to the substance and essentiality of a right and its protection from future legislative changes.

If changes of this nature are to be admitted, they must pass the so-called proportionality test[10] (which has long been applied to restrictions of "fundamental rights" by the German constitutional doctrine) and therefore, they must be necessary, adequate, and temporary (or caused by extraordinary circumstances).

---

[10]For further developments see: Sobek and Montag (2019).

Tomáš Sobek and Josef Montag have clarified the origins of the "proportionality test" as follows: "*After the Second World War, the German constitutional theory developed the proportionality test as its main methodological tool for reconciling conflicting rights and values. Proportionality test is a method that allows courts to structure the decision dilemma at hand in a way that facilitates the decision to be carried out in a rational and transparent manner by balancing the benefits and costs – broadly understood – of alternative courses of action. And this approach proved to be viable. The proportionality test, indeed, became a dominant technique of adjudication of hard cases around the world.*"[11]

Another author, Panagiotis Souliotis, on the same subject:

> To begin with, the principle of proportionality is a legal construction. It is a tool for the judges to reconcile the clashing interests in human rights conflicts or in human rights against public interest conflicts and to find a solution which respects the human rights and the private interests of the individual and, simultaneously, cares for the promotion of the public interests and the protection of the public order (ordre public). It is described as a criterion which focuses on the appropriate correlation which must exist between the aims and the means.[12]

Also, as Eva Gröninger-Voss[13] pointed out, "protection of acquired rights" is an essential principle which aims at striking a delicate balance between the competing needs of IO's (international organisations) to adapt their functioning and employment conditions to evolving circumstances and, at the same time, ensure personnel have stability of employment conditions and to be protected against arbitrary change and erosion. It is based on the recognition that international civil servants do not participate in a democratic legislative process in relation to their salaries and entitlements and, thus, require enhanced protection.

Features of employment relationships, imbalance of power between employer and employee and the essentiality of salary in that context, renders the application of the principle of acquired rights, in this context, particularly sensitive while justifying a "proportionality test."

In Judgement UNDT/NBI/2020/106, the first instance tribunal of the United Nations made the following assertions:

> (…) consideration must be given to the fact that the employment relation presupposes continuality and durability, whether during a predetermined finite period or indefinitely, with salary playing a central role in it. Periodical render of salary does not transform employment into a series of consecutive contracts where each subsequent one could be renegotiated. Another consideration must be given to inherent inequality of the parties and the socio-economic function of salary as a source of maintenance, thus giving reason for a specific protection by law. Yet another consideration is due to the fact that the employment relation, and especially in civil service, presupposes equivalence of service and the counter-performance; downward amendment of remuneration distorts this equivalence. All these concerns speak in favour of protection against unilateral and unfettered downward revision of salary to extend throughout the duration of service.

---

[11] *Idem.*

[12] See, Souliotis (2015), pp. 1–26.

[13] See, Gröninger-Voss et al. (2017), *idem*.

While we maintain that international organisations need to have some margin of discretion to change, review and adapt salaries and entitlements of their staff, particularly, in times of economic or financial crisis (lack of funding and / or restructuring processes) there is a need to balance those needs against the fundamental nature of salaries, in the context of an employment relationship.

IOs have a duty of care towards their staff and the changes to be implemented cannot be of such gravity as to breach the mutual trust and good faith that is at the core of the employment relationship.

5 Conclusion

The jurisprudence of ILOAT, UNDT, UNAT and the World Bank's Administrative Tribunal show the evolving nature of international administrative law and how different institutions deal with similar concepts.

Although each international organisation has its own internal set of rules, regulations, procedures and administrative practices it is possible to identify commonly adopted concepts and legal principles which are cross-sectorial. This is due to "cross-fertilisation" and the dialogue international administrative tribunals and appeals board establish among themselves.

Nonetheless, despite this common dialogue and frequent exchanges among legal professionals and institutional actors, some jurisprudential divergences have emerged in recent years.

Contrary to what was commonly accepted by practitioners, and scholars, the concept of acquired rights was not "set in stone" and the 2018 UNAT judgement has clearly demonstrated that jurisprudence can always depart from the original consensus and introduce disruptive solutions.

"Judicial disruption" can have some beneficial effects as it demands creative solutions from legislators and decision-makers but, at the same time, it can also have a negative impact on the fragile balance of interests between staff members and high senior management.

From accountability point of view, civil society must monitor how international organisations and their (internal) administrative tribunals deal with challenges and address "hard cases."

Jurisprudence is a barometer that shows how IOs' employment relations work and whether they can (still) fill the mandate member states granted them.

Jurisprudence

ILOAT

- Plissard, Judgement No. 12 (1954)
- Sheriff, Judgement No. 29 (1957)
- Lindsey, Judgement No. 60
- Settino, Judgement No. 426 (1980)

- Ayoub, Judgement No. 832 (2017)
- Judgement No. 4134 (2018)

UNAT

- (former) United Nations Administrative Tribunal (Judgement No. 19, Kaplan)
- (former) United Nations Administrative Tribunal (Judgement No. 273, Mortished, 1981)
- (former) United Nations Administrative Tribunal (Judgement N. 1253, Ittah, 2005)
- 2018-UNAT-840
- 2021-UNAT-1108

UNDT

- UNDT/GVA/2017/097
- UNDT/NBI/2020/106

WBAT

- De Merode /decision.1/ June 5/1981

Electronic resources

- https://documentsddsny.un.org/doc/UNDOC/GEN/N15/458/91/PDF/N1545891.pdf?OpenElement
- https://www.un.org/internaljustice/oaj/en
- http://lnweb90.worldbank.org/crn/wbt/wbtwebsite.nsf/(resultsweb)/470F6C6098A11FDF852569ED006BB877 [5/20/2014 11:54:49 AM]

References

Gröniger-Voss, E., Kristen Baxter, A., & Nguyen Dao, A. (2017). The principle of acquired rights with particular focus on the jurisprudence of the Administrative Tribunal of the International Labour Organization. In D. Petrovic (Ed.), *90 years of contribution of the Administrative Tribunal of the International Labour Organization to the creation of international civil service law* (pp. 109–128). ILOAT.

Gulati, R. (2021). *Acquired rights in International Administrative Law*. Max Planck Yearbook of United Nations Law Online, 17 December 2021, pp. 82–109.

Sobek, T., & Montag, J. (2019). Proportionality Test (February 19, 2018). In A. Marciano & G. B. Ramello (Eds.), *Encyclopedia of law and economics*. Springer.

Souliotis, P. (2015). *Proportionality and the European Convention on Human Rights. A critical view* (pp. 1–26). Grinn., available online at; https://papers.ssrn.com/sol3/papers.cfm?abstract_id=2690366

Institutional Setting of Administrative Tribunals: The Case of the Inter-American Development Bank Administrative Tribunal (IDBAT), with References to Its Peers

Giuliana Canè

Contents

1 Introduction 15
2 Members of the Tribunal 17
2.1 Qualifications 17
2.2 Selection and Length of Term 19
2.3 Contract and Emoluments 20
2.4 Jurisdiction *Ratione Personae* and *Ratione Materiae* 21
3 The Secretariat of the Tribunal 24
3.1 Introduction and Overview 24
3.2 Transparency to Enhance Accountability 26
3.3 Transparency to Better Assist Potential Users of the Tribunal 29
4 Conclusions 34
Statues and Rules 34
Bibliography 36

1 Introduction

International organizations are often granted functional immunity, including immunity from jurisdiction, to operate more efficiently and be capable of reaching their institutional goals.

Giuliana Canè, lawyer, Executive Secretary of the Inter-American Development Bank Administrative Tribunal.

G. Canè (✉)
Executive Secretary of Inter-American Development Bank Administrative Tribunal, Washington, DC, USA
e-mail: giulianac@iadb.org

T. Bravo, K. Bradley (eds.), *Judicial Review in International Administrative Law*, Law for Professionals, https://doi.org/10.1007/978-3-031-71840-3_2

Internal grievance mechanisms, and administrative tribunals, have been set up as a counterbalance to this jurisdictional immunity.[1] After operating for a couple of decades these mechanisms often need to be re-examined and assessed to make sure they still perform their original function of providing an independent judicial forum which is a valid alternative to the domestic jurisdiction for employment-related issues that may be raised by staff, thus safeguarding the institutions' immunity where they operate.

To maintain the immunity from jurisdiction granted to many international institutions by their founding instruments, these organizations have over time modified the internal grievance systems in two directions: first, by making them more effective and capable of resolving disputes at the earliest possible stage; and second, by increasing the independence and thus the credibility of their mechanisms of last resort, the administrative tribunals.

As an example of the first direction, in 2009 the United Nations introduced mediation in the informal system by replacing its peer review bodies, the Joint Appeals Boards (JABs), by a Management Evaluation Unit and a two-tier judicial system consisting of the United Nations Dispute Tribunal (UNDT) and the United Nations Appeals Tribunal (UNAT). Either party may now challenge a UNDT judgment before the UNAT.[2]

A recent change was implemented in the IDB system in early November 2022, when the President *a.i.* announced the consolidation of the Office of Ombudsperson and the Office of Mediation into the Office of Ombuds and Mediation Services (OMN) to reinforce the IDB conflict resolution mechanisms, providing more services designed having in mind the employee's perspective. The new OMN will serve as a one-stop shop for employees to access ombuds and mediation services in a more direct and efficient manner.[3]

This chapter analyzes the second direction, i.e., the characteristics of the features of the IDBAT that strengthen its independence, by analyzing the independence of its members (the judges) and the independence of the Secretariat, the internal IDB office that functions as a bridge between the Tribunal and the institution and that guarantees the day-to-day continuity of the Tribunal's work. The chapter will focus primarily on how the provisions of the Statute and the Rules of Procedure[4] work in practice, and how each instrument could affect the independence of the Tribunal's work.

---

[1] Additional reasons for the establishment of administrative tribunals are, for example, to allow a uniform interpretation of the internal law of the institution by one judicial organ (instead of many possible tribunals of member countries); to provide a timely resolution of the claim; and to avoid multiple ramifications of the same claim in various local courts.

[2] See https://www.un.org/en/internaljustice/overview/about-the-system.shtml. Accessed on 15 July 2024.

[3] https://www.iadb.org/en/who-we-are/transparency/office-ombuds-and-mediation-services.

[4] Rules of Procedure of the Administrative Tribunal of the Inter-American Development Bank Group, last amended on May 1, 2024, available at www.iadb.org/tribunal.

2 Members of the Tribunal

The independence of the members of the Tribunal is ensured by several safeguards including their qualifications, selection, contracts, emoluments, and term of office.

2.1 Qualifications

The Statute specifies: "Members of the Tribunal shall be persons of recognized professional competence and integrity who have the necessary qualifications to occupy a similar position in the highest judicial courts of their countries or who are jurisconsults of recognized competence. Members of the Tribunal shall not be selected from current or former Bank or Corporation Employees, nor shall they be eligible to become Employee(s) of the Bank or the Corporation, or provide services to third parties in connection with initiatives of the Bank or the Corporation within five years after having been members of the Tribunal."[5]

The Rules determine the number of members and the mode of appointment, but practice adds other key elements when determining the specific composition. For example, geographic diversity is not mandated by the IDBAT Statute, as it is by the ILOAT Statute, where "due regard shall be given to geographical distribution and gender balance in the composition of the Tribunal."[6]

In practice, however, the IDB Tribunal has always included a U.S. national, a national from one of the Central American countries, a national from one of the Caribbean countries, and a national from a Southern Cone country. Regional representation is not a written rule, but it is often respected; 46 members have been appointed from member countries in the region (22 regional borrowing member countries and two regional non-borrowing member countries), of 54 members overall (see Fig. 1). This outcome reflects both the share of each member country's

[5] Article III of the Statute of the Administrative Tribunal of the Inter-American Development Bank Group is available at www.iadb.org/tribunal. A similar requirement is established by many tribunals. See, for example, the IMF Statute, Article VII(1)(c): "The members shall have no prior or present employment relationship with the Fund, must be nationals of a member country of the Fund at the time of their appointments and must possess the qualifications required for appointment to high judicial office or be jurisconsults of recognized competence." Available at https://www.imf.org/external/imfat/statute.htm. See also the World Bank Tribunal, Article IV(1) "... The members of the Tribunal shall be persons of high moral character and must possess the qualifications required for appointment to high judicial office or be jurisconsults of recognized competence in relevant fields such as employment relations, international civil service and international organization administration," available at https://tribunal.worldbank.org/; and the ILOAT Statute, Article III.1: "The Tribunal shall consist of seven judges who shall all be of different nationalities. The judges shall be persons of high moral character, impartiality and integrity and must have been appointed to, or possess the qualifications required for appointment to, the highest judicial office of their countries," available at https://www.ilo.org/tribunal/about-us/WCMS_715861/lang%2D%2Den/index.htm.

[6] ILOAT Statute Article III.1, available at https://www.ilo.org/tribunal/about-us/WCMS_715861/lang%2D%2Den/index.htm.

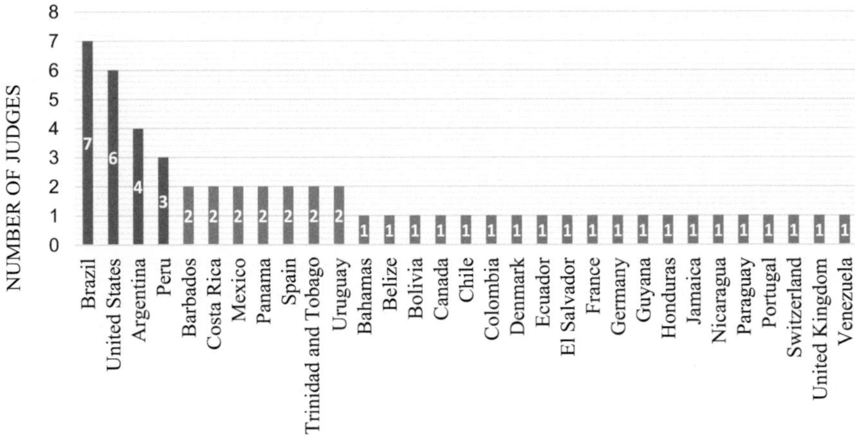

Fig. 1 Tribunal judges by nationality (1981–2024) (*The Administrative Tribunal of the Inter-American Development Bank Group: Taking Stock of its Four Decades of Jurisprudence*, graph 1, p. 14, updated to 2024 for this article, available at www.iadb.org/tribunal)

contribution (with the United States being the largest shareholder) and the criteria of proportionality and rotation. Having seven members on the Tribunal allows for a broader representation, applying the various criteria.

Additionally, the composition has reflected an unwritten rule whereby both common law and civil law traditions are represented on the Tribunal.[7] The same is true at the Administrative Tribunal of the OAS, which also has judges from both the common law and civil law systems.

Another criterion not explicitly mandated by the Rules but ever more respected in practice is a gender balance between male and female professionals serving on the Tribunal.

As data show that women are still significantly underrepresented in decision-making positions in all fields, although they make up at least half of the population,[8] it would be desirable to have gender balance in the composition of the administrative tribunals. Historically, of the 54 members of the IDB Tribunal, 72% have been male, while only 15 members have been female. Indeed, the appointments of the last decade have sought to correct this imbalance, as since 2014, the majority of the Tribunal's members have been female judges (see Fig. 2).

---

[7] Augustin Gordillo, La justicia administrativa internacional, Chap. XVI, available at chrome-extension://efaidnbmnnnibpcajpcglclefindmkaj/https://www.gordillo.com/pdf_tomo2/9ed/capitulo16.pdf

[8] The European Commission, available at https://commission.europa.eu/strategy-and-policy/policies/justice-and-fundamental-rights/gender-equality/equality-between-women-and-men-decision-making/achieving-gender-balance-decision-making_en#women-and-men-in-economic-decision-making.

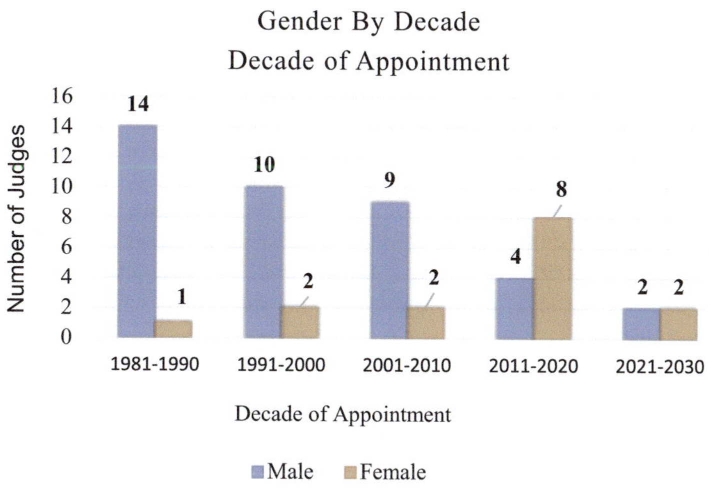

Fig. 2 Tribunal judges by gender (1981–2024) (*The Administrative Tribunal of the Inter-American Development Bank Group: Taking Stock of its Four Decades of Jurisprudence*, graph 4, p. 15, updated to 2024 for this article, available at www.iadb.org/tribunal)

2.2 Selection and Length of Term

Before the last amendment, in 2013,[9] the judges were appointed by the Bank's Board of Executive Directors: four were elected from lists proposed by Bank Management, while three were chosen from lists put forward by the Staff Association. They were appointed for three years and could be re-elected once.

Currently, Article III of the Statute of the Administrative Tribunal ("the Statute")[10] provides that the Tribunal's members are appointed by the Board of Executive Directors from a list of candidates presented to it by a Nominating Committee for the Administrative Tribunal established as provided in Annex I to the Statute. The seven members must be nationals of member countries, with no more than one national from the same country at the same time.

The recruitment process starts in practice with the publication of the notice of vacancy on the IDB website. Each candidate applies directly.[11] The Nominating Committee, consisting of five members,[12] holds as many meetings as may be

[9]Resolution DE-11/13, adopted on February 27, 2013.

[10]The Statute of the Administrative Tribunal of the Inter-American Development Bank Group is available at www.iadb.org/tribunal.

[11]In other organizations, member countries play a greater and more direct role in the nomination of the tribunal's judges as they directly propose candidates or need to endorse candidacies (for example, at the ILO and OAS tribunals).

[12]The five members of the Nominating Committee are: the Chairperson of the Organization, Human Resources and Board Matters Committee (OHRA Committee) of the Bank; one staff member of the Bank appointed by the President of the Bank; one staff member of the Corporation appointed by the

necessary to fulfill its functions. Once the Nominating Committee has conducted all the necessary interviews it proposes two names of candidates for each vacant post, first to the OHRA Committee, and then to the Board of Executive Directors at large.[13]

The Board of Executive Directors appoints members of the Tribunal for one non-renewable term of six years.[14] The terms are staggered so that the composition of the Tribunal maintains continuity; accordingly, there are always senior members when new members come on board.[15] The 2013 amendment strengthened the independence of the Tribunal: having a longer non-renewable term encourages the members to decide based only on the law and their conscience, with no thoughts of a possible second term.[16]

2.3 Contract and Emoluments

Another aspect of the term of office of the members of the Tribunal that can enhance their independence is the amount of compensation and the mechanics of how it is paid.[17] Various solutions could potentially be chosen: judges could be reimbursed

General Manager of the Corporation; and two staff members appointed by the Staff Association. Typically, one professional from the Human Resources Department and one from the Legal Department sit on the Committee.

[13] Annex I to the Statute, para 5.

[14] As a point of comparison, the World Bank Statute at Article IV(3) provides for a term of five years with the possibility or one additional five-year term; the OAS Statute mandates (Article III(3)) a six-year term with a maximum of two consecutive terms in office; according to the UNAT Statute (Article 3(2)), the members are appointed by the General Assembly for four years and may be reappointed once; at the IMF (Article VII(2)) members are appointed for four years for a maximum of two additional terms; the Asian Development Bank Tribunal's Statute states (Article IV(3)) that the members of the Tribunal are appointed for a period of three years and may be reappointed by the Board of Directors, upon the recommendation of the President, for a maximum of two further terms of three years each.

[15] Every two years two new members join the Tribunal and every six years three new members join on July 1.

[16] "The possibility exists that the judge may favour the organization in the hope or expectation of his term being renewed. It is not whether he does or does not that matters but whether it is possible, or there is a temptation, for him to do so... The solution is to have one non-renewable term." Amerasinghe (2003), p. 246.

[17] The remuneration level is one of the factors that affect the independence of the Tribunal. According to C. F. Amerasinghe "salaries or fees must be fixed clearly (a) at the beginning of a judge's tenure and (b) at such a level as is reasonable, taking into account all the relevant circumstances or factors, including the fact that the office is judicial and not of any other kind, which implies the recognition of qualities such as dignity and authority, and particularly the general level of salaries or fees of judges in the international legal system and, (c) most importantly, must be at such a level as is conducive to and preserves the independence of the judges and does not jeopardize it." See Amerasinghe (2003), p. 246.

only for their travel expenses to attend Tribunal sessions at IDB headquarters ("HQ"), while volunteering their time; they could be paid per hour of work billed;[18] or they could be awarded a fixed amount per year, independent of the caseload in any particular year.

The IDB chose the last-mentioned solution, determining a fixed emolument per year, paid in two installments. The amount is unrelated to the hours of work performed in that particular year.

Some detractors point out that the fixed amount is a generous payment, especially in years when the Tribunal does not have new or pending cases. The reality is that while the amount could be generous in the first year of service of a new member—as new members are inevitably less involved in cases already pending as of the date when they join the Tribunal[19]—the reverse is true at the end of their term of office when senior members serve as President of the Tribunal and their involvement in the Tribunal's current matters is weekly and significantly greater than that of the other members.

Having fixed emoluments set up front, and that cannot be decreased during their term of office,[20] simplifies and clarifies administrative dealings with the Secretariat and reduces possible discrepancies among members of the Tribunal, reducing the possibility of brokering on the amount of work necessary in a particular case.

2.4 Jurisdiction *Ratione Personae* and *Ratione Materiae*

Article II of the Statute lists the employees who have access to justice before the Tribunal: "Employee," which means "any current or former person appointed by the Bank or of the Corporation in accordance with its employment practices to render services as an employee, and who receives regular remuneration from the Bank or the Corporation (including consultants) including retired staff members receiving a pension from the Plan, or any person who is entitled to present a claim upon a right of such current, former, or retired staff member. . . ."[21]

---

[18] For example, this is the method chosen for the World Bank judges. According to Amerasinghe: "Judges of the WBAT are paid approximately at the rate of $250 per hour ($1500 for a six-hour working day) for work done, which is comparable to legal fees in the US legal sector." In Amerasinghe (2002), Chap. 15, p. 323, footnote 18. This amount is revised periodically.

[19] In practice, the IDBAT tries to conclude pending cases before new members join the Tribunal: once the oral arguments have been heard, and often even earlier in the procedure, once the hearing of witness testimony has taken place, the Tribunal composition does not change, even if there is no rule precluding it from doing so, to give continuity to the decision-making process for the benefit of the parties.

[20] See, for example, the ICJ Statute, Art. 32(5) "These salaries, allowances, and compensation shall be fixed by the General Assembly. They may not be decreased during the term of office." Available at https://www.icj-cij.org/statute.

[21] Article II of the IDBAT Statute, available at www.iadb.org/tribunal.

Thus, the main criterion for referring claims to the Tribunal is that the complainant needs to have a direct contract with the institution, no matter whether the contract is for staff position, with an indefinite term, or temporary, as in the case of consultants. The Statute did not limit jurisdiction to certain grade levels, nor did it exclude certain categories (such as, for example, members of the Board of Executive Directors, or professionals in trust positions), although the system has yet to be tested in these latter categories.

As for the scope of the review, Article II of the Statute clarifies that the Tribunal hears and passes judgment upon any "application by which an Employee of the Bank or of the Corporation alleges non-observance of his or her contract of employment or terms and conditions of appointment" and that "the words 'contract of employment' and 'terms and conditions of appointment' include all pertinent regulations and rules in force at the time of the alleged non-observance, including the rights or benefits established by a Bank Staff Retirement Plan."

Based on the wording of Article II and the Tribunal's case law it seems that staff may challenge any administrative decision affecting them, including decisions implementing general rules, and that when doing so they may also challenge the legality of the underlying general rule. One matter which has not yet come before the Tribunal is the possibility of challenging a general rule without the staff member waiting for a specific decision that directly affects them. The Statute is silent in this regard, unlike more explicit provisions, for example, the statutes and rules of procedures of the IMF[22] and EBRD[23] administrative tribunals.

The Tribunal's scope of review is generally limited to the party's claim, and it will not take the place of the administration, as it has reiterated in various judgments.[24] Yet at the same time, the administration's discretion is subject to limitations, for example, respect for due process and protection from abuse of authority or arbitrariness.[25]

[22]The Statute of the Administrative Tribunal of the IMF, Article II(2) states: "For purposes of this Statute: a. the expression 'administrative act' shall mean any individual or regulatory decision taken in the administration of the staff of the Fund; b. the expression 'regulatory decision' shall mean any rule concerning the terms and conditions of staff employment, including the General Administrative Orders and the Staff Retirement Plan, but excluding any resolutions adopted by the Board of Governors of the Fund. . . ." Available at https://www.imf.org/external/imfat/statute.htm. Accessed on 15 July 2024.

[23]EBRD Appeals Procedures, Article 1.03 states that "'Administrative Decision' means an Individual Decision or Regulatory Decision taken by the Bank in the administration of the staff of the Bank; where the Bank is required to act within a specified time period pursuant to the Terms and Conditions of Employment of a Staff Member and fails to do so, an Administrative Decision is deemed to have been taken as a result of such failure."

[24]See, for example, Judgment, Case 103, TD v. IDB (2022), para 82: "Although the Tribunal cannot substitute its judgment for the evaluation of a staff member, it finds it extremely surprising that a staff member who produces good quality work could be terminated for unsatisfactory performance on the basis that her output was allegedly untimely." Available at www.iadb.org/tribunal.

[25]Judgment, Case 100, BD v. IDB (2022), paras 38 and 39; Case 88, Irene Guimarães Altafin et al. v. IDB (2017], para 94, both available at www.iadb.org/tribunal.

In addition, the Tribunal will give indications that go beyond the matter at stake when it finds that a particular issue is recurring and could lead to inequality of arms between the parties. For example, the Tribunal signaled[26] that the procedure for consulting confidential documents could erode the principle of equality. Article 18(2) of the Rules of Procedure ("the Rules")[27] provides for an *in-camera* procedure whereby "when the parties provide information they regard as confidential, they shall specifically so inform the Executive Secretary. The Member presiding over the proceedings, having consulted the other Members of the Tribunal or panel, shall determine whether the information so submitted can be regarded as confidential. The Executive Secretary shall safeguard this evidence and shall make a record of it in the case file. The parties may examine this evidence only in the office of the Secretariat of the Tribunal."[28]

The confidential nature of a document may be relied upon a party (mostly by the respondent) and tends to follow a broad definition in line with the IDB's access-to-information policy. However, the access-to-information policy indicates whether and when a document will be disclosed to the public, while the confidentiality of a document during the discovery phase should be interpreted narrowly, as the parties to a case are bound not to use such a document outside of the proceedings.

Bearing this context in mind, "the Tribunal is concerned about the restricted access and the effects that this could have on the ability of counsel to prepare adequately in bringing complaints to the Tribunal. While the Tribunal did not find evidence on record sufficient to support a breach of the principle of equality in this case, it does emphasize the importance of the principle."[29]

Another signal can be found in a recent decision[30] where the Tribunal, asked by the complainant to issue a supplemental judgment on an already-decided case, included an obligation for the respondent to provide the Tribunal with a report on the implementation of the judgment within three months of the date of issuance. This indication was deemed appropriate after a series of requests by the complainants in various cases already closed, triggered by an alleged lack of prompt and full compliance with the judgments. The Tribunal, in a plenary session, then decided to clarify the issue, amending its Rules and adding a new Article 28 [now Article 16(3) in the new Rules] whereby "within ninety calendar days of the date the judgment or other decision is issued, unless a different time limit is specified in the Judgment or in the Statute or Rules of Procedure of the Tribunal, each party shall

[26] Case 88, Irene Guimarães Altafin et al. v. IDB (2017), para 95, available at www.iadb.org/tribunal.

[27] Article 18 of the new Rules of Procedure, approved on May 1, 2024. Please refer to similar provision of previous Rules of Procedure of the Administrative Tribunal of the Inter-American Development Bank Group, Article 28, last amended in 2022, available at www.iadb.org/tribunal.

[28] Article II of the IDBAT Statute, available at www.iadb.org/tribunal.

[29] Case 88, Irene Guimarães Altafin et al. v. IDB (2017), para 95, available at www.iadb.org/tribunal.

[30] Supplemental Judgment, Case 104, Viviana Vélez-Grajales v. IDB [2022], para 6, available at www.iadb.org/tribunal.

carry out the corresponding actions ordered by the Tribunal and shall, on or before the expiration of that period, notify the Tribunal and the other party or parties in writing of the actions taken."[31]

3 The Secretariat of the Tribunal

3.1 Introduction and Overview

To operate, the Administrative Tribunal needs to have a permanent office or secretariat, even if a small one, incorporated in the institution it serves.

In keeping with the independence and autonomy of the Tribunal, the characteristics of the IDBAT Secretariat and its staff could support or undermine the overall role of an administrative tribunal within a given institution.[32]

It is proposed to take a closer look at how the Secretariat is designed, its role and place in the overall institution, and the mechanisms put in place to increase the transparency and accountability of its work and that of the Administrative Tribunal vis-à-vis the staff and the Board of the institution, and it is intended to possibly serve as a point of reference for its users and peers.

At the time of writing the IDBAT Secretariat is made up of an Executive Secretary (or registrar),[33] a paralegal, a financial officer, and an assistant. These functions are now performed by regular staff.[34] Until a few years ago, the Secretariat had only one regular staff member (the financial officer), while all other functions were performed by professionals with consultant contracts. Since abundant case law by various administrative tribunals, including the IDBAT, has made it clear that staff-like functions should be performed by regular staff,[35] the case was made before the Board of Executive Directors to open the corresponding job positions, without requesting any additional budget.

[31] Rules of Procedure of the Administrative Tribunal of the Inter-American Development Bank Group, last amended on May 1, 2024, available at www.iadb.org/tribunal.

[32] "The registry . . . needs to be considered in the context of the fundamental principle of law relating to independence of the judicial organ. While the registry is not part of the bench of judges of the judicial organ, it is part of the judicial organ. . . . The fundamental principle of law is, as stated earlier, that the independence of the judicial organ be preserved, respected and ensured, not merely that of the bench of judges" Amerasinghe (2003), p. 246.

[33] I have had the pleasure of serving in this role since January 2016.

[34] Although IATs generally benefit from a secretariat or a structure that assists them in the day-to-day tasks, the human resources assigned to these secretariats are often employed on a part-time basis (either as external consultant or because only 50% or their time is assigned to the work of the Tribunal). Having full-time staff assigned to the tribunal makes it possible to have a deeper impact on the institution in question, as it enables it to focus not only on the judicial activity, but also on data analysis and outreach.

[35] Jorge O. Amora v. Asian Development Bank, Decision No. 24 (1997); Case 80, Elba Agusti, R. Anne Vena, Felipe Verdejo-Sancho et al. v. IDB (2015).

The role of the Secretariat is such that the professional leading the office needs to maintain a certain distance from the institution where he or she sits. Depending on the type of structure created, the Secretary, while structurally being a staff member of the institution, needs to maintain functional and practical independence, and therefore distance, from the institution to which he or she belongs, and particularly from Management itself, as it is a party in all cases before the Tribunal. Some safeguards might be already included in the terms of appointment, such as the fact that candidates may not include current or former employees of the institution, the maximum length of contracts (ten years), the reporting line, and performance evaluations.

In practice, the Secretary should avoid any perception of bias. For example, while it is the right of every employee to belong to the Staff Association and take advantage of its services, it is advisable to choose not to do so if one is serving as Secretary. Indeed, the Staff Association can appear as an *amicus curiae,*[36] and can provide complainants legal or financial support even without appearing in a specific case.

This functional arms-length distance from the institution might create a certain isolation in the work of the Secretary, yet engaging with other players might be necessary and healthy. One of the venues for exchanging ideas and comparing notes is the international network that is being formed by the offices of executive secretaries of the administrative tribunals in international organizations around the world. Besides affording the possibility of quickly reaching out to colleagues with questions and exchanging experiences by email, this group used to meet in person every year for informal discussions on topics of common interest. At present the network covers about 20 such tribunals.[37] The recent establishment of new tribunals[38] has created further possibilities for exchange and for assisting the newer tribunals in the natural struggle to preserve their independence and existence, especially vis-à-vis the very authorities that set them up.

[36] Article 24 of the IDBAT Rules of the Procedure, as amended on May 1, 2024, states: "The Tribunal may permit any person or entity with a substantial interest in the outcome of the case to participate as a 'friend-of-the-court'. In particular, it may permit the duly authorized representative of the Staff Association of the Bank, or of the Corporation, to do so." Available at www.iadb.org/tribunal.

[37] For a then complete list of IATs, see "The Contribution of International and Supranational Courts to the Rule of Law: A Framework for Analysis," Geert De Baere, Anna-Luise Chané, and Jan Wouters, in de Baere and Wouters (2015), p. 20, footnote 5.

[38] In the last year or so, a number of new tribunals came into function, namely: the Caricom Administrative Tribunal, SKAO (Square Kilometer Array Organization); the OPEC Fund Administrative Tribunal, and the CABEI (Central American Bank for Economic Integration) Administrative Tribunal.

3.2 Transparency to Enhance Accountability

Transparency and accountability need to be put in place for the work of both the Tribunal (mainly judgments and final orders) and the Executive Secretariat, which ensures the operations of the Tribunal. Transparency and accountability increase employees' trust in the independence of the Tribunal.

Several tools have been put in place in recent years to ensure transparency and accountability in the work of the IDBAT.

3.2.1 Request for an Audit Report

To respect the independence of the office, institutions might hesitate to include the Secretariat of the Tribunal among the units to be audited on a regular basis. In this context, it might be appropriate to voluntarily request to be included in the list of units subject to audit, especially after a management transition and change in leadership at the Secretariat. This would make it possible to leverage the good experiences of past management and potential recommendations for needed corrections.

For example, one of the recommendations of the audit report that was voluntarily requested in 2016 has been to align the Administrative Tribunal staff and consultants with other staff when it comes to logging hours and leave time in the Bank's official time reporting system, since the previous exception to Bank policy was not justified by the stated aim. Historically, the staff of the IDBAT Secretariat used to be considered subject to only some of the Bank's policies and procedures on administrative matters, and not to others, such as the use of the administrative budget, procurement, travel, human resource management, and information and file management. The reason given was that this would enable the unit to avoid any unnecessary scrutiny or undue control over day-to-day matters by Management. The audit made the change possible.

3.2.2 Web Page of the Tribunal: Same Page Internally and Externally

The website of an organization is the main tool for communicating with an unidentified audience that could potentially become its users. The same is true for the IDBAT: the website is now conceived of as a key tool of communication for both its internal audience (employees, the Staff Association, the Human Resources Department, and the Board of Executive Directors) and its external audience (former employees, retirees, or any person who is entitled to present a claim upon a right of a current, former, or retired staff member), with no difference in content. This solution, which has some limitations—for example, hearings for oral argument are public only for employees of the IDB, thus the dates of such hearings are not published on the website, to avoid any confusion as to who could attend—is nonetheless optimal for guaranteeing a level playing field between current and former employees of the IDB, who are all potentially able to file a complaint with the IDBAT.

3.2.3 Publication of Judgments and Summaries in English

Although historically the IDBAT's decisions were published on the Tribunal website, they were not easily searchable: only a list of decisions was made available from which was not possible to search the case law without knowing the exact number of the case. The stated reason for this rigid way of publishing was to protect the people involved (complainants and witnesses); yet if you were to put the names of the complainants or other words in an internet search engine, the full decision appeared immediately. The system was both ineffective for its intended goal and not user-friendly for those who needed to consult the case law of the IDBAT.

Now, all judgments are searchable on the main page of the Tribunal (www.iadb.org/tribunal) under the heading "Decision." The search includes criteria such as year, case number, and name of the case.

Publishing the judgments on the website is only the first step to increasing the transparency of the Tribunal's case law: it would not be realistic to think that employees or potential users of the Tribunal's services read all the decisions. The relevant question is: How can the Tribunal's case law be made more accessible to the public and to other tribunals?

One possible step in this direction is undertaking an analysis, by topic, of all the judgments issued by the Tribunal.

A "Digest," which includes a search via keywords such as "contract of employment," "fixed-term contract," "dismissal," "discrimination," and "abuse of authority." This effort entails summarizing all the decisions, categorizing them by main groups (such as contract of employment, disciplinary measures, selection process, staff retirement plan, violation of the code of ethics, and revision) and subgroups (for example, under contract of employment there will be fixed-term contracts and renewals, performance evaluation/merit salary increase, promotions, salary review adjustment, tax reimbursement, termination, time limits for filing complaint). A summary of each decision is then be labeled with keywords (which will be searchable in the search engine). In developing the keywords, we considered not only the terminology used by the IDBAT, but also the most common terminology used by similar tribunals. This is to facilitate the search for both internal and external audiences.

Besides being used as a search engine this **Digest**[39] is also published as a standalone document, whose objectives include facilitating access to specific topics examined by various decisions, notwithstanding the terminology used in the judgments,[40] simplifying referencing recent and earlier case law, and facilitating

[39] IDB Tribunal Case Digest 1981–2022 available at www.iadb.org/tribunal

[40] One of the challenges to accessing the case law of the IDBAT has been that the terminology used over time and across languages (as per Article 22(2) of the Rules of Procedure, "The judgments of the Tribunal shall be issued in Spanish and English;" in practice the Tribunal issue a decision in one language—either English or Spanish- and then the text is translated) varies significantly. Additionally, although in practice members of the IDBAT tend to have at least a working knowledge of Spanish and English, this is not a prerequisite established in the Statute, as for instance in the case of the ILOAT, where Article III.1 expressly requires that "They must have an excellent knowledge of

comparison of the IDBAT's caselaw with the other administrative tribunals when they have addressed the same topic.

3.2.4 Budget

Historically, the Tribunal's budget has been part of the operational budget presented by Management to the Board of Executive Directors. In other words, the budget of the Secretariat of the Tribunal was not an individual line item for which the independent office was accountable to the institution. In fact, Management was not conducting detailed reviews of the Secretariat's expenses to avoid the impression of interfering with the judicial function. More recent changes proposed by the Secretariat have been to make the Tribunal a separate line item and to report to the Board, annually, on the specific budget approved and executed. In addition, accountability and improved planning made it possible to operate from fiscal years 2017–2020 with a 0% nominal increase, absorbing the market-based salary increase (MBSI), as approved by the Board of Executive Directors. Since fiscal year 2021, the Secretariat reduced its budget proposal by 10.10%, considering the economic impact of the COVID-19 pandemic and its implications for the Management of the IDB Group in its mission to improve lives and promote social and economic development in the member countries of the region.

3.2.5 Annual Reports

Reporting to shareholders and stakeholders on the main activities performed and how the budget has been executed is one of the key accountability features of any organization.

Starting in 2016, the IDBAT Secretariat took the initiative to report on its activities and budget expenditures to the IDB Board of Executive Directors. What started as a point under "other items" on the Board agenda is now a regular semi-annual presentation scheduled in the agenda, eagerly awaited by the shareholders.[41] On the occasion of the presentation of the Annual Report, several bilateral meetings are scheduled with different Executive Directors: these are moments where the dialogue with the Board, the representative of the ultimate owners of the institution, is enhanced and regular feedback is provided on the main issues.

Starting with the Annual Report for 2019, these reports have been published on the Tribunal's website, ensuring accountability vis-à-vis the stakeholders as well.

The Annual Report normally covers highlights of (1) judicial activities, such as how many decisions have been issued and main updates (for example, the

at least one of the working languages of the Tribunal and should also have at least a basic written and oral comprehension of the other working language.... At all times the Tribunal's composition shall permit the Tribunal to render judgments in both working languages."

[41] Typically, the IDBAT Secretariat presents the Annual Report of its previous calendar year of activities in May, while it presents the Work Plan and Budget proposal for the following year in October.

introduction of an electronic system for filing the complaint and other pleadings)[42]; (2) outreach activities (such as specific presentations to groups of employees, onboarding presentations, videos, and publications)[43]; and (3) budget execution.[44]

3.3 Transparency to Better Assist Potential Users of the Tribunal

Potential users of the Tribunal often experience an asymmetry of information compared with the respondent institution: they do not necessarily have access to the internal rules applicable to them; they are not always literate in legal terminology, nor are they always able to navigate the various internal grievance mechanisms made available to them by the institution; and they might choose to represent themselves without availing themselves of the advice of a lawyer.

3.3.1 User-Friendly Tools

To try to balance out this asymmetry, as part of its public function the Secretariat has developed some user-friendly tools in recent years. The very first was a flyer on "**Frequently Asked Questions,**"[45] which compiled the 27 questions most frequently heard from colleagues during the first few open house events. The responses mostly provide a practical sense of how the Tribunal works. One of the most frequently asked questions is whether complainants must be represented by an attorney, and what the cost of such representation might be. Another frequent question is whether a complainant may request anonymity in the proceedings.

A second instrument introduced is the **Step-by-Step Guide**, which graphically illustrates the three phases (pleadings phase, evidentiary phase, and deliberation phase) and the various actions to be performed by each party.[46]

---

[42] To preserve the independence of the judicial function, the Annual Report does not go into the merits of cases decided. This solution preserves the integrity of the function of the Secretariat as conceived in its founding act, see the double reporting line of the Secretariat, established by Article V of the Statute (to the Board for administrative issues, and to the members of the Tribunal for judicial activities).

[43] It is increasingly accepted that the new generation of international courts "has taken on new roles, which indicate not only a quantitative but also a qualitative change in the international judiciary. Whereas international courts were traditionally only mandated with dispute settlement between states, today they fulfil multiple functions, including ... the promotion of the development of international law" Geert De Baere, Anna-Luise Chané, and Jan Wouters "The Contribution of International and Supranational Courts to the Rule of Law: A Framework for Analysis," in de Baere and Wouters (2015), p. 22.

[44] The practice when it comes to publishing annual reports varies among tribunals, with a recent change by the Asian Development Bank Administrative Tribunal. Following the amendment to its Rules of Procedure, adopted by the Tribunal on February 10, 2021—whereby under Rule 3 (Duties of President and Vice-President) "the President shall prepare an annual report on the activities of the Tribunal, which shall be published"—the first report was published in 2022. Available at https://www.adb.org/documents/administrative-tribunal-annual-report-2021. Accessed on 15 July 2024.

[45] *Frequently Asked Questions,* available at www.iadb.org/tribunal.

[46] *Step by Step Guide,* available at www.iadb.org/tribunal.

As the composition of the Board of Executive Directors changes in part every July, some members of the Board arrived at the first presentation of the Work Program of the Secretariat of the Tribunal without any familiarity with how the Tribunal operates, why and when it was constituted, and who can bring a case before it. The Secretariat developed a **Brief Introduction to the Administrative Tribunal** for their benefit[47]; it has come to be widely used outside of the institution as well, by peer organizations and scholars.

One of the characteristics peculiar to the IDB procedures is that oral proceedings (witness testimony or oral argument hearings) are normally conducted in each case. This is not the practice at some other administrative tribunals, where oral proceedings are not permitted, not requested, or not held at all. While holding a hearing has an impact on the length and cost of the proceedings before the Tribunal, it also provides the complainants their "day in court," their only chance to interact with the Tribunal when their case is being considered.[48] This is the rationale for the practice of holding hearings before the IDB Tribunal. In fact, the IDB Tribunal has held hearings for oral arguments in more than 90% of the cases that reached a final decision. By way of comparison, the IMF Tribunal held oral hearings in about 5% of its cases, the World Bank Tribunal in about 3% of its cases, and the OAS Tribunal in about 58% of cases. Hearings are rare before the ILOAT and the UNDT, mainly due to the large number of cases decided every year by these tribunals. To explain this procedural feature, and to provide detailed comparative data, the Secretariat has published the article entitled **Oral Hearings in the Procedures and Practices of the IDB Group Administrative Tribunal.**[49]

While the analytical pieces are tools often consulted by counsel and professionals already familiar with the activity of the Tribunal, the general public often finds it more enjoyable to hear from the judges themselves and other users through brief **video interviews** on topics that come up during the various town halls and open houses hosted by the Tribunal. Videos are now available on the Tribunal's website on the experience of the users, colleagues, and peers; on serving on the Administrative Tribunal; on the Tribunal's effort to reduce factors that might prevent access to the service it provides; and similar topics.[50]

---

[47] *A Brief Introduction to the Administrative Tribunal,* available at www.iadb.org/tribunal.

[48] Pustorino (2023), p. 161: "Among the other rights that apply to the various judicial proceedings falling within the scope of the right to a fair trial is the right of the litigants to have their dispute discussed and decided in public hearings, so that the proceedings are conducted in a manner which is visible and accessible to the public, in order to preserve the relationship of trust between the national community and the administration of justice. However, reasons of efficiency and economy of judicial proceedings, security, protection of particularly vulnerable individuals or other reasons based on objective justifications may exclude or limit, also with regard to certain stages of the proceedings, the application of this specific guarantee."

[49] *Oral Hearings in the Procedures and Practices of the IDB Group Administrative Tribunal,* available at www.iadb.org/tribunal.

[50] Videos now available are: The experience of the users; The experience of colleagues and peers; The experience of the judges; Serving on the Administrative Tribunal of the IDB Group; Challenges

As the Tribunal is the final instance in the IDB Group whose decisions are binding, staff members must know when to use it, the steps that must be exhausted before filing a complaint, and the relevant deadlines. Accordingly, in May 2021 the Secretariat launched an **online course**, mandatory for staff and consultants.[51] In just two months, it was completed by 96% of IDB Group employees and it is now part of the mandatory courses for new employees.

3.3.2 Data Analytics

The legal profession and courts around the world are in the midst of a transformative period in which data analytics and other deep-learning technologies can have a profound impact on their work. Mining data gives them a competitive advantage and insights to better serve their audience.

Embracing this mindset, the Secretariat has embarked on an overall classification of all past case law according to common pre-established criteria, such as date of filing, nationality of the party, type of contract, and job position at the time of the filing, whether the party had the assistance of counsel, requests for extension per case, and date of hearing. After the database was compiled, the team identified emerging legal trends.

The initial analytical investment has been fruitful on two fronts: first, to help users easily identify whether an issue has been already dealt with, or whether there is a trend in the outcomes of specific kinds of claims; and second, to flag potential issues that cannot be identified by looking at an individual decision.

For example, by analyzing the case law we noticed that the vast majority of the complainants were holding a regular staff contract at the time of the filing. The last amendment of the Statute in 2013 ratified a Tribunal practice[52] whereby all employees, including consultants, who have a direct contractual relationship with the Bank could bring a case before the Tribunal. As of July 2024, the composition of Bank personnel was approximately 2260 staff and 1630 consultants working for the IDB Group at HQ and in the Country Offices ("COFs"); however, only about 2%[53] of professionals with consultant contracts had filed cases with the Tribunal (see Fig. 3). Thanks to this data analysis the Secretariat designed an internal communication campaign specifically targeting professionals hired as consultants. Although a

---

and achievements of the Tribunal during the pandemic and after a year of working remotely; The Tribunal's effort to reduce factors that may prevent employees from accessing its service.

[51] Instructional videos that are part of the mandatory course are now available for everyone interested at the Tribunal's website, namely: Introduction; The Tribunal's Operational Framework; Composition of the Administrative Tribunal; Procedure for Filing the Complaint: Pleadings Phase; Procedure for Filing the Complaint: Probative Phase; Procedure for Filing the Complaint: Deliberation and Judgment Phase.

[52] The Tribunal had previously accepted jurisdiction over a consultant in Case No. 70, NT v. IDB (2009), available at www.iadb.org/tribunal.

[53] Please refer to Graph 16 "Complainants by type of contract" in *The Administrative Tribunal of the Inter-American Development Bank Group: Taking Stock of its Four Decades of Jurisprudence*, available at www.iadb.org/tribunal.

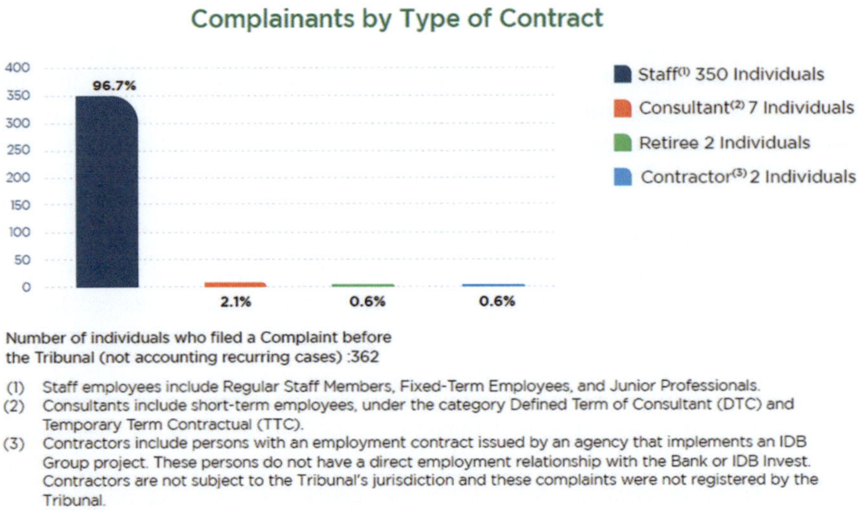

Fig. 3 Complainants by type of contract (*The Administrative Tribunal of the Inter-American Development Bank Group: Taking Stock of its Four Decades of Jurisprudence*, graph 16, p. 25, available at www.iadb.org/tribunal)

direct causal link between the number of cases and contractual modality cannot be established, circumstantial evidence shows that lack of information or fear of retaliation were possible reasons for the low number of consultants filing cases. As a result, the Secretariat now systematically offers tools to better serve this segment of the staff population, such as information sessions and onboarding presentations where those present are mostly consultants.

As another example, data analysis indicated that almost two-thirds of the complainants (64%) were stationed at HQ, while the rest were working in a country office (mainly Brazil, Bolivia, Argentina, and Chile) at the moment of filing a complaint. Although two-thirds is also roughly the share of the personnel stationed at HQ compared to those based at the Bank's 28 country offices (COFs) from which the Bank operates, prima facie this data was not meaningful per se. Analyzing these latter cases in detail, we noticed that the complaints from country offices tended not to be individual but rather collective, regarding mainly the interpretation of internal policy or a local application of a Bank policy to local staff (see Fig. 4).[54]

This last point also suggested to us the potential need to fill an information gap with a communication campaign that could facilitate knowledge-sharing on how to access the Tribunal services, mainly targeting colleagues in COFs.

[54] As examples of cases filed by multiple complainants stationed in different country offices, please refer to Cases 86, 87, and 89, Rudi Luis Cressa et al., María Cecilia Ares et al., Karen Allison Canterbury et al. v. IDB (2017); see also Case 88, Irene Guimarães Altafin et al. v. IDB (2017), both available at www.iadb.org/tribunal.

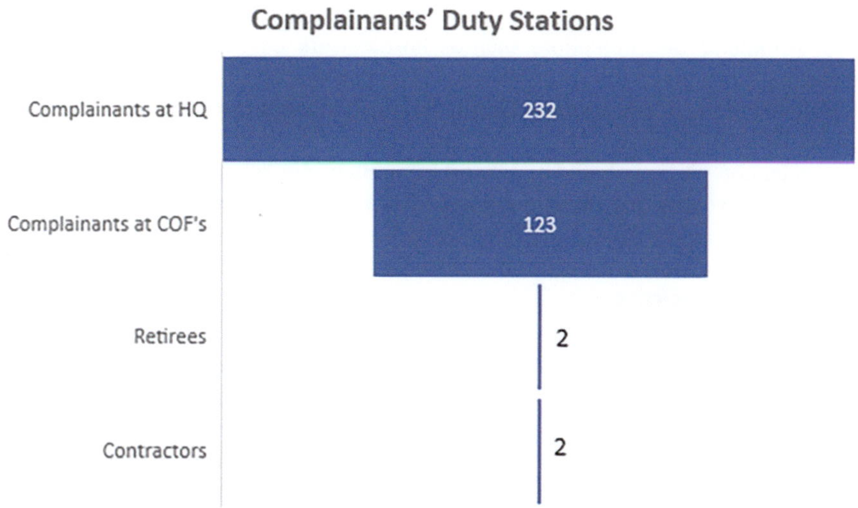

Fig. 4 Complainants' duty stations (*The Administrative Tribunal of the Inter-American Development Bank Group: Taking Stock of its Four Decades of Jurisprudence,* graph 17, p. 26, available at www.iadb.org/tribunal)

The analysis of cases raising discrimination and harassment claims is another example of how data can shed light on trends not easily identifiable through the analysis of individual decisions.

The institution makes it clear by various means that discrimination in the workplace will not be tolerated,[55] and data show that of the 120 judgments issued by the IDBAT from 1982 to 2022, only about 10% of the complaints included an allegation of discrimination; the discrimination allegation was the primary claim in less than half of these. Similar findings can be analyzed for harassment claims, which have been made in about 10% of the cases that ended in judgments; in most of those cases, the claims pertained to workplace harassment and were not the primary claims.

One possible explanation is that the institution tries to resolve or settle allegations of discrimination or harassment at the earliest opportunity, without letting the matter reach the Tribunal. A prompt resolution of the case could preserve the employment relationship. Another possible explanation for the limited number of cases on discrimination and harassment could be fear of retaliation.[56]

[55]For example, Provision 9 of the IDB Code of Ethics and Professional Conduct (2012) states: "The Bank respects and values the diversity reflected in our various backgrounds, experiences, and ideas. Maintaining a workplace free of discrimination is a paramount duty that we all share. We must be dedicated to providing an inclusive work environment that fosters respect for all of our coworkers, clients, and business partners, and one that reflects the diversity of the communities in which we operate. We do not wrongfully discriminate against anyone on the basis of nationality, race, gender, religion, age, sexual orientation, disability, social status, or political orientation."

[56]The IDB expressly prohibits acts of retaliation against any person who has or is suspected to have reported prohibited practices in Bank-financed activities or misconduct to Bank authorities in good

Examining the type of discrimination alleged in detail, the primary concern has been workplace discrimination, such as hostile work environment and abuse of authority, followed by discrimination based on national origin or ethnicity.[57]

Another element that came to light is that several cases based on discrimination claims were filed jointly by several complainants,[58] suggesting that the alleged discrimination was rule-based and that the complainants, while asking the Tribunal to rectify their individual situations, were also seeking a policy change for others.

4 Conclusions

When a professional starts an employment relationship with an international organization, the last concern is what happens if the relationship is compromised. This is especially the case when the employment relationship brings the professional aboard in a new country, which implies making a series personal choices and adjustments. However, differences among co-workers or between the workers and the institution are natural during the span of a career and cannot always be avoided.

The Tribunal and its Secretariat contribute to maintaining a healthy and respectful working environment while also clarifying and interpreting the legal framework for resolving labor-management disputes. By increasing transparency and accountability the Administrative Tribunal provides the institution and its staff the assurance that its role is balanced and neutral and allows for the staff's engagement in the core projects of the institution in client countries.

Statues and Rules

IDB Resolution DE-11/13, adopted on February 27, 2013

IDB Statute of the Administrative Tribunal of the Inter-American Development Bank Group, 2014

IDB Rules of Procedure of the Administrative Tribunal of the Inter-American Development Bank Group, 2024

EBRD Appeals Procedures

faith. See Provision 4.3 of the IDB Code of Ethics and Professional Conduct (2012) and Staff Rule PE-328, "Whistleblower Reporting and Protection."

[57] A similar finding of few cases alleging discrimination, most of which pertain to workplace discrimination, has been reported in a comparative analysis of the case law of the Asian Development Bank in a recent publication by Trebilcock (2022), pp. 1–16, doi:10.1017/S2044251322000182.

[58] See, for example, Case 5, Jacques Cook et al. v. IDB (1982) on the issue of national income tax; Cases 86, 87, and 89, Rudi Luis Cressa et al., María Cecilia Ares et al., Karen Allison Canterbury et al. v. IDB (2017), on access to benefits for local versus international staff; Case 88, Irene Guimarães Altafin et al. v. IDB (2017), on salary condition of local versus international staff; Case 80, Elba Agusti, R. Anne Vena, Felipe Verdejo-Sancho et al. v. IDB (2015), on alleged violation of the principle of equality and the principle of equal benefits for equal work.

IMF, Administrative Tribunal of the International Monetary Fund, 2020
Asian Development Bank: Statute of the Administrative Tribunal of the Asian Development Bank
OAS Statute of the Administrative Tribunal
World Bank Administrative Tribunal, Statute and Rules, 2020
ICJ Statute

IDB Cases

1. Case 9 Tula Amas v. IDB [1986]
2. Case 23 Buria-Hellbeck v. IDB [1989]
3. Case 32 Mariana Renart v. IDB [1992]
4. Case 34 Castañeda v. IDB [1993]
5. Case 35 Vega v. IDB [1993]
6. Case 42 Peroustianis v. IDB [1996]
7. Case 43 Quintero v. IDB [1997]
8. Case 70, NT v. IDB [2009],
9. Cases 86, 87, and 89 Rudi Luis Cressa et al., María Cecilia Ares et al., Karen Allison Canterbury et al. v. IDB [2017]
10. Case 88, Irene Guimarães Altafin et al. v. IDB [2017]
11. Case 100 BD v. IDB [2022]
12. Case 103 TD v. IDB [2022]
13. Supplemental Judgment Case 104 Viviana Vélez-Grajales v. IDB [2022]

Other cases

1. International Court of Justice **Effect of Awards of Compensation Made by the United Nations Administrative Tribunal,** July 13, 1954, Advisory Opinion: incompatibility with the Charter
2. International Court of Justice **Judgments of the Administrative Tribunal of the ILO Upon Complaints Made Against UNESCO ICJ,** October 23, 1956, Advisory Opinion, ICJ Reports (1956), 77: competence of UNAT
3. **Chadsey**, October 15, 1968, (ILOAT Case 122): right of access to a court
4. **Mullan v. Secretary General of the United Nations** Judgement No. 162 (October 10, 1972)
5. United States Court of Appeals, District of Columbia Circuit **Broadbent v. Organization of Am. States** 628 F.2d 27 (D.C. Cir. 1980): undercutting immunity
6. **De Merode v. The World Bank**, Decision No. 1, June 5, 1981.
7. United States Court of Appeals, D.C. Circuit **Mendaro v. The World Bank** 717 F.2d 610 (D.C. Cir. 1983): US court
8. **Rubio**, July 10, 1997, (ILOAT Case1644), right of access to a court
9. **UNESCO v. Boulois,** Tribunal de grande instance de Paris (ord. Réf.), October 20, 1997, Rev. Arb. (1997) 575; Cour d'Appel Paris (14e Ch. A), June 19, 1998: France

10. European Court of Human Rights **Waite and Kennedy v. Germany** [1999] ECHR Application No. 26083/94 "reasonable alternative means," right of access to a court
11. UNAT Judgement No. 941 Case No. 1026: **Kiwanuka** Against: The Secretary-General of the United Nations, November 19, 1999
12. Brussels Labour Court of Appeal (fourth chamber), **Siedler v. Western European Union**, September 17, 2003, Journal des Tribunaux (2004), 617, ILDC 53 (BE 2003), Belgium
13. Italian Supreme Court **Pistelli v. European University Institute** Corte di Cassazione, Sezioni Unite Civili, October 28, 2005, No. 20995: Italian Court
14. French Cour de Cassation, **Banque africaine de développement v. M.A. Degboe, France**, January 25, 2005
15. Italian Corte Di Cassazione Case No. 3718 **Drago v. International Plant Genetic Resources Institute (ipigri)** February 19, 2007: Italian Court
16. **Tissa Amaratunga v. Northwest Atlantic Fisheries Organization**, a body corporate 2013 SCC 66
17. **Budha Ismail Jam et al. v. International Finance Corporation**, United States Court of Appeals, June 23, 2017, No. 16-7051

Bibliography

Amerasinghe, C. F. (1994). The law of the International Civil Service (Vols. I and II).

Amerasinghe, C. F. (2002). International Administrative Tribunals, Chapter 15.

Amerasinghe, C. F. (2003). Principles of the Institutional Law of International Organizations.

Best Practices in resolving employment disputes in International Organizations, Conference hosted by the International Labour Office, September 2014.

Cançado Trindade, A. A. (2015). Prologue: An Overview of the contribution of international tribunals to the rule of law.

de Baere, G., & Wouters, J. (2015). The contribution of international and supranational courts to the rule of law.

IDB Tribunal Case Digest 1981-2022 available at www.iadb.org/tribunal.

Pustorino, P. (2023). Right to liberty and security, right to a fair trial and principle of no punishment without law. In *Introduction to International Human Rights Law*. T.M.C. Asser Press. https://doi.org/10.1007/978-94-6265-563-8_8

Trebilcock, A. (2022). Approaches to discrimination claims: A comparison of the Administrative Tribunals of the Asian Development Bank and the Inter-American Development Bank Group. *Asian Journal of International Law, 2022*, 1–16. https://doi.org/10.1017/S2044251322000182

Legal Standing Before (International) Administrative Tribunals and the Role of Staff Associations

Teresa Bravo

Contents

1 Introduction 37
2 Staff Associations and Employment Relations in International Organisations 38
3 *Locus Standi* Before Internal Justice Systems and Receivability *Rationae Personae* 41
4 Former Staff Members and the Requisite of "a *Nexus* with the Previous Employment Relationship" 42
5 Access to Justice for Judges and Other Elected "Officials" in the UN 43
6 Access to Justice for Non-Staff Members in the UN Internal Justice System 46
7 Legal Standing and the Role of Staff Associations 47
8 Staff Associations as *Amicus Curiae* in Judicial Proceedings 49
9 Conclusion 51
Jurisprudence 52
Electronic Resources 52
Reference 52

1 Introduction

Legal standing before international administrative tribunals or appeal boards is a fundamental part of access to justice in the context of international organisations since these institutions benefit from legal personality and jurisdictional immunity.

Teresa Bravo, Judge and former President of the UNDT, Judge at the IADBAT and Asian Development Bank Administrative Tribunal

T. Bravo (✉)
United Nations Dispute Tribunal, Lisbon, Portugal

T. Bravo, K. Bradley (eds.), *Judicial Review in International Administrative Law*, Law for Professionals, https://doi.org/10.1007/978-3-031-71840-3_3

Therefore, legal standing should be understood as an umbrella concept that comprises a set of requirements and conditions, under which staff members in international organisations can have access to internal justice systems.

Establishing who has access to internal appeal mechanisms is not only a legal option but also a political one, due to its potential impact on the mandate and functioning of the institution, its managerial and administrative practices, and, ultimately, on its own budgetary procedures and regulations.

Legal standing before internal justice mechanisms is a prerogative of staff members but the evolving nature of international administrative law has changed this scenario and an increased call for a broader and open access to justice is taking place.

One of the main challenges is whether to include staff associations in these internal justice mechanisms and grant them the appropriate *locus standi* to represent their associates in "collective actions" against the organisation when regulatory decisions are at stake.

This chapter addresses the status of this debate while considering internal rules and regulations, as well as the jurisprudence of two major international actors, namely ILOAT and UNAT to understand if and how staff associations can, indeed, play an active role in the context of international organisations' justice systems.

2 Staff Associations and Employment Relations in International Organisations

On 04 October 2022, all staff associations in the UN Secretariat wrote a letter to the Secretary-General expressing their dissatisfaction with the content of a proposal made by the SG in its Annual Report on the Administration of Justice[1] in relation to a provision to be included in the Statute of the United Nations Dispute Tribunal (hereinafter, the UNDT) that would limit the need for a hearing and reverse the burden of proof in disciplinary cases.

The underlying rationale of said proposal was, according to the SG's Report, that recent judgements "fail to respect the role of the Secretary-General, who under Article 97 of the Charter is the chief administrative officer of the United Nations and has been entrusted by the General Assembly in staff regulation 10.1 with the authority to impose disciplinary measures on staff members who engage in misconduct."[2]

From the administration's point of view, there is a need to clarify the scope of review to be conducted by the Tribunals in disciplinary cases. Consequently, the Secretary-General proposed the following addition to the statute of the Dispute Tribunal:

[1] See SG Report A/77/156, issued on 19 July 2022. Accessed on 23 July 2024, available at https://documents.un.org/doc/undoc/gen/n22/423/53/pdf/n2242353.pdf?token=23Qf4k9FlYvASQe88Y&fe=true.

[2] See para 127.

Article 9

4. In hearing an application to appeal an administrative decision imposing a disciplinary measure, the Dispute Tribunal shall pass judgment on the application, determining whether the decision was a reasonable exercise of the Secretary-General's authority based on the evidence before the Secretary-General at the time the administrative decision was taken. The applicant shall bear the burden of showing that the decision was not a reasonable exercise of the Secretary-General's authority.

This proposed addition to the UNDT's statute, which was included without previous consultation with staff members or judges, has raised concerns in the UN system about limiting the scope of judicial review and launched a discussion on the role of staff associations in the policy-making of international organisations and what sort of participation can staff associations have in those internal justice systems.

The letter signed by the Presidents of all Staff Unions and Associations presented at the Staff Management Committee has raised red flags as follows:

The undersigned Presidents of all the United Nations Secretariat Staff Unions and Associations represented at the Staff Management Committee (SMC) wish to place on record our deepest alarm and firm objection to the narrative and proposed amendment to the Statute of the Dispute Tribunal contained in paras 121–128 of report A/77/156 on Administration of Justice at the United Nations. Our objections are both of a procedural and substantive nature.

The Staff Unions are available to engage in consultation on all matters related to the integrity, effectiveness and credibility of disciplinary proceedings, through the channels established under Chapter VIII of the Staff Regulations and Rules, as well as in a manner that is inclusive of all non-Secretariat organizations that also come under UNDT/UNAT jurisdiction.

It is clear from this letter that something is changing within the UN system and staff associations are no longer willing to let proposals made by the administration (such as this one) be approved by the General Assembly without having the opportunity to make suggestions or amendments since multilateralism, pluralism and consultations are at the core of the UN's mandate and enshrined in the UN culture.

Nonetheless, it is fair to say that a large majority of international organisations, if not all of them, do not recognise the legal standing of staff associations but only to individual staff members (even when regulatory decisions are at stake) and the role of said associations is often limited to that of *amicus curiae* in legal proceedings.

Employment relations in the UN system are unique because UN staff do not have a single employer: they are employed by all 193 Member States that make up the UN. As international civil servants work for an international organisation, they are not protected by any national labour laws or international conventions, as these do not apply to them. Although freedom of association is enshrined in most of the staff regulations of the UN and the various specialised agencies forming the UN common system, national trade unions are not recognised.[3]

[3] See ILO Staff Union, consulted online on 06 August 2024 at https://ilostaffunion.org/en/about-staff-union/news.

Working conditions are negotiated directly with each international directorate, while conditions of employment (salaries, benefits, job classification and others) common to the entire UN common system are reviewed globally by a UN technical body, the ICSC (International Civil Service Commission), which submits its recommendations to the fifth Committee of the UN General Assembly representing the Member States. All UN staff unions and associations are represented by umbrella federations (FICSA, CCISUA and UNISERV), but have no real negotiating power within the ICSC. Moreover, staff unions or staff associations (contrary to what happens in municipal systems) do not have legal standing in the internal justice system of international organisations.[4]

In this regard, it is worth mentioning the key concept allowing access to tribunals or internal appeal bodies—receivability *ratione materiae*—is the concept of "administrative decision" which is defined as a decision taken by the competent administrative authority in an individual and specific case which has a direct impact in the terms of appointment or the contract of a staff member.[5]

Thus, administrative decisions are distinguished from other administrative acts, such as those having regulatory force (which are usually referred to as rules or regulations), as well as from those not having direct legal consequences. Administrative decisions are, therefore, characterised by the fact that they are taken by the administration, they are unilateral and of individual application, and carry direct legal consequences.

In the United Nations legal system, the Appeals Tribunal has adopted a pragmatic approach in reviewing various types of challenges that involve decisions of general application, seeking to identify the exact nature of the challenge being brought.

It evaluates, on a case-by-case basis, whether staff members were effectively challenging the legality of a decision taken by a regulatory body such as the General Assembly or the ICSC (see, e.g., *Tintukasiri et al.* 2015-UNAT-526; *Kagizi* et al. 2017-UNAT-750 and *Reid* 2015-UNAT-563), or whether the staff members are asserting a different cause of action stemming from a violation of their individual terms and conditions of employment as a result of the implementation of the regulatory measure in their individual cases (see, e.g., *Ovcharenko et al.*[6] and *Pedicelli*[7]).

For instance, in *Pedicelli,* the Appeals Tribunal stressed that the substantive argument put forward by the Applicant was that the implementation of the new seven-level salary scale promulgated by the ICSC "affected her contractual rights under her permanent appointment" (see para 30).

---

[4] Idem.

[5] See the definition of administrative decision as per *Andronov* jurisprudence (2003-UNAT-1157).

[6] Judgement No. 2022-UNAT-1262, accessed on 09 August 2024 at https://www.un.org/internaljustice/oaj/en/judgment/2022-unat-1262.

[7] Judgement No. 2015-UNAT-555, accessed on 09 August 2024 at https://www.un.org/en/internaljustice/files/unat/judgments/2015-UNAT-555.pdf.

In *Tintukasiri et al.*, the Appeals Tribunal held that the Tribunal "can incidentally examine the legality of decisions with regulatory power, [but] it does not have the authority to rescind such decisions."

In the internal legal systems of international organisations, the case law refers specifically to individual decisions but experience has shown that regulatory decisions impacting several individuals in different institutional settings have also been (indirectly) challenged before internal justice mechanisms.

Therefore, the question remains: who can challenge those decisions and how?

In the next paragraphs, the current status of this debate will be further highlighted and discussed.

3 *Locus Standi* Before Internal Justice Systems and Receivability *Rationae Personae*

International organisations have been granted jurisdictional immunity to be able to fulfil their mandates without any political or external interference from member states and host countries. One of the features of this immunity is the fact that staff members of these organisations cannot seek redress of their grievances before national courts.

Nevertheless, to ensure access to justice, they are entitled to seek review of administrative decisions taken by their employer before an independent internal organ.

To protect staff member's rights, international organisations have established processes for review of staff grievances that comply with general principles of fairness and due process.

Under Article 3 of the United Nations Dispute Tribunal, only staff members, former staff members and a person making a complaint on behalf of an incapacitated or deceased staff member can file an application before the UNDT.

Throughout the years, UNAT and UNDT's jurisprudence has not departed from the established internal rules and instead, a restrictive and conservative approach to legal standing has been adopted.

For instance, in its judgement UNDT/GVA/2015/118 (*Fikri)*, a case in which a UN contractor appealed a UNOPS decision, the Tribunal stated that:

> (...) it results from the provisions above that the Tribunal has jurisdiction only over applications filed by a staff member, a former staff member or a person making claims in the name of an incapacitated or deceased staff member, with respect to an administrative decision that is alleged to be in non-compliance with the terms of appointment or the contract of employment.
>
> 10. The above quoted sec. 6 of the Applicant's contractor agreement unambiguously provides that the Applicant's legal status was that of an independent contractor, which "shall not be regarded, for any purpose, as a staff member of UNOPS or any other entity of the United Nations ... under the Staff Regulations and Rules of the [United Nations]."
>
> 11. It follows that, as an individual contractor, the Applicant was not a staff member and, therefore, the application is not receivable, ratione personae (cf. Ghahremani 2011-UNAT-171).

In international working settings a diversity of contractual liens may co-exist.

This diversity is encompassed by restrictions on access to internal justice systems and leads to an imbalance of power among co-workers, supervisors, and supervisees. An imbalance of power may fuel work-related conflicts and harassment, since those in a more fragile legal position or with a weaker contractual link will tend to be silent in the face of abusive conduct and refrain from making complaints.

These reasons may justify equal access to the internal justice system irrespective of the nature of the contractual lien with the organisation.

4 Former Staff Members and the Requisite of "a *Nexus* with the Previous Employment Relationship"

In *White* 2021/UNDT/089, the UNDT has adjudicated as irreceivable *ratione personae*, a complaint made by a former UN staff member who was separated from service on 23 March 2019 and was contesting the administration's decision of 23 April 2021 to declare him ineligible as a candidate for a position and excluded him from the recruitment process.[8]

This was not an innovative decision but instead a reiteration of a former jurisprudence that constitutes now well-settled case law of the UN internal system (see also *Shkurtaj* 2011-UNAT-148, para 29).

In this judgement, the Tribunal recalled Art. 3.1(b) of its statute, which allowed a former staff member to file an application under Art. 2.1 concerning, inter alia, an administrative decision "that is alleged to be in non-compliance with the terms of appointment or the contract of employment" or "imposing a disciplinary measure."

However, the UNDT highlighted that a former staff member has standing to contest an administrative decision before the Tribunal only if there is *"a sufficient nexus between the former employment and the contested decision"* and that *"[a] sufficient nexus exists when a decision has bearing on an applicant's former status as a staff member, specifically when it affects his or her previous contractual rights"* (see *Arango* 2021-UNAT-1120, para 28; see also *Shkurtaj* 2011-UNAT-148, para 29).

In addition, the Tribunal explained that:

> 16. In the present case, the Applicant applied as an external candidate for JO 136410 more than a year after his separation from the Organization. At the time of the contested decision, he had been separated from service for more than two years. In his application, he does not assert any right acquired in terms of his previous contract of employment with the Organization. Instead, he challenges as an external candidate the Administration's decision to declare him ineligible for a position based on his age. This decision had no bearing on his former employment in the sense that it affected any contractual rights he had acquired under it. The Tribunal is thus of the view that there is no nexus between the Applicant's former employment and the contested decision.

[8] See White, UNDT/2021/089, accessed on 23 July 2024 at https://www.un.org/internaljustice/oaj/en/judgment/undt2021089.

17. Further, the Tribunal recalls that its limited jurisdiction in relation to persons implies that it "ordinarily will not have authority to receive applications by inter alia job applicants alleging illegality, unfairness or discrimination in the recruitment process" (see Arango 2021-UNAT-1120, para 28).

18. Accordingly, the Tribunal finds that the Applicant does not have standing and the application is not receivable ratione personae.

However, this was not the only case in which the UN internal legal system has clarified the limits and scope of "receivability *ratione personae*" and the issue of legal standing.

The absence of a *forum* in the UN system for judges to present their grievances against the administration will be addressed in the next chapter. This is an unfortunate situation as it represents, in our view, a serious *deficit* in already established international standards of judicial independence.

5 Access to Justice for Judges and Other Elected "Officials" in the UN

In 2019, the Appeals Tribunal confirmed a first instance judgement in which the UNDT had rejected an application filed by a former *ad litem* judge at the International Criminal Tribunal for the former Yugoslavia (ICTY) who had filed a complaint against a decision of the Registrar of the ICTY, not to pay him for his part-time service in that Tribunal, after he was appointed to the International Criminal Court (ICC) as a judge, (see *Mindua 2019-UNAT-921).*[9]

The rationale of the underlying decision was based on the UNDT's statute which restricts judicial review to staff members.

The UNDT Statute

Article 2(1)(a) of the UNDT statute provides that the UNDT is competent to hear and pass judgment on an application filed by an individual as provided for in Article 3(1) of the UNDT statute.

Article 3(1) in turn provides that an application under Article 2(1) may be filed by any staff member or former staff member of the United Nations, including the United Nations Secretariat or separately administered United Nations funds and programmes, or any person making claims on behalf of any such staff member who is deceased or incapacitated.

The UNDT's jurisdiction *ratione personae* is, accordingly, limited to these three categories of applicants. Their jurisdiction is narrowly defined and leaves a number of individuals working for the Organisation without access to the internal justice system due to the specific and precise definition of "staff member."

[9] See 2019-UNAT-921, accessed on 23 July 2024 at https://www.un.org/internaljustice/oaj/en/judgment/2019-unat-921.

Staff members of the United Nations are appointed under Article 101(1) of the Charter of the United Nations (the Charter) which states: "The staff shall be appointed by the Secretary-General under regulations established by the General Assembly."

Staff Regulation 4.1 confers the power of appointment of staff members upon the Secretary-General, while Staff Regulation 1.2(c) subjects staff members to the authority of the Secretary-General.

Thus, to be a staff member, the individual concerned must be appointed by the Secretary-General through a letter of appointment issued in terms of Staff Regulation, as was held in *Basenko v. Secretary-General of the United Nations*, Judgement No. 2011-UNAT-139.

In that case, the Applicant had been elected as an *ad litem* judge of the ICTY by the General Assembly on 24 August 2005. The posts of *ad litem* judges of the ICTY were established under Resolution 1329 (2000) of the Security Council, which resolved to establish a pool of *ad litem* judges and to that end amended Articles 12, 13 and 14 of the statute of the ICTY.

In terms of Article 13quarter of the ICTY statute, *ad litem* judges of the ICTY were elected by the General Assembly from a list submitted by the Security Council after the Secretary-General had invited nominations from Member States of the United Nations and non-member States maintaining permanent observer missions at the United Nations Headquarters.

The President of the Security Council then transmitted the list of candidates to the President of the General Assembly. From that list, the General Assembly elected twenty-seven *ad litem* judges for a term of four years. The elected *ad litem* judges were eligible for re-election.

Therefore, the procedure for the appointment and election of judges is totally different from the one for appointing staff members. Article 13quarter of the ICTY statute provided that during the period of their appointment, *ad litem* judges were entitled to the same terms and conditions of service *mutatis mutandis* as the permanent judges of the ICTY.

The terms and conditions of service of the permanent judges were stipulated by Article 13bis (3) of the ICTY statute to be those of the judges of the International Court of Justice.

In said judgement, UNDT stated that: "The *ad litem* judges, being elected by the General Assembly, were thus not appointed by the Secretary-General and enjoyed the same terms and conditions of appointment determined by the General Assembly in terms of Article 32 of the Statute of the International Court of Justice. The *ad litem* judges were also not subject to the general authority of the Secretary-General."

In addition, the Tribunal clarified that staff members are held accountable before the SG and can even be subject to disciplinary sanctions in cases of misconduct, which does not happen to the judges.

Staff Regulation 1.3 specifically provides that staff members, who are accountable to the Secretary-General for the proper discharge of their functions, are required to uphold the highest standards of efficiency, competence and integrity in the discharge of their functions, and their performance will be appraised periodically to ensure that the required standards of performance are met. None of these requirements apply to judges; nor should they, as they would amount to unacceptable limitations upon judicial independence.

Moreover, in Resolution 61/262, adopted on 4 April 2007, the General Assembly, with the ICTY in mind, explicitly reaffirmed the principle that the conditions of service and compensation for non-Secretariat United Nations officials shall be separate and distinct from those for officials of the Secretariat. Judges of the organisation are clearly intended to be officials, other than Secretariat officials and are thus not staff members.

Nonetheless, that does not mean that judges do not have obligations and duties as elected officials. Indeed, ST/SGB/2002/9 (Regulations Governing the Status, Basic Rights and Duties of Officials other than Secretariat Officials, and Experts on Mission) records that the United Nations has persons performing full-time services for it, at the direction of its legislative organs, who are not staff.

For example, Article 13 of the Statute of the Joint Inspection Unit (approved by the General Assembly in its Resolution 31/192 of 22 December 1976) provides that the Inspectors shall have the status of officials of the organisation but shall not be staff members. Those persons are usually the presiding officers of United Nations organs performing functions for the organisation on a substantially full-time basis but are referred to as "officials other than Secretariat officials."

The UNDT therefore concluded that the Applicant was not a staff member as he had not been appointed by the Secretary-General in terms of Staff Regulation 4.1 and was not subject to his authority. He had been elected by the General Assembly.

UNAT confirmed this argument and concluded that the UNDT did not err in dismissing the application as not receivable *ratione personae.*

UNAT and UNDT's jurisprudence must be distinguished from the ILOAT's case law in this regard.

Indeed, in a case in which the complainants were two former judges of the ICC who raised issues before the ILOAT about their pension entitlements, the Respondent/ICC contended that the complainants lacked legal standing to bring the complaints to that Tribunal.

However, the ILOAT held that Article II, para 5, of its statute expressly provided that it is competent to hear complaints alleging non-observance, in substance or in form, of the terms of appointment of "officials" of any other international organisation (including the ICC) recognising the jurisdiction of the ILOAT.

The ICC did not dispute that the complainant judges were officials of the ICC and consequently, it had in law recognised the ILOAT's jurisdiction to determine disputes regarding judges' benefits.

The ILOAT's jurisdiction *ratione personae*, therefore, is broader than the UNDT's jurisdiction in that it may be invoked by "officials," which the ILOAT held includes judges.

The UNDT's jurisdiction, by contrast, is limited to "staff members," a narrower category because when the General Assembly defined the scope of the UNDT's jurisdiction, it specifically considered and rejected proposals to include non-staff personnel.

The General Assembly has, in turn, emphasised that the Tribunals shall not have powers beyond those statutorily conferred on them. If the current situation violates the norms of customary international law, as it appears to be, it is a matter for the General Assembly, and not for the Tribunals, to rectify.

In the alternative, judges in the UN system may have to file applications before the ILOAT, if they are faced with an illegal decision affecting their terms of appointment.

6 Access to Justice for Non-Staff Members in the UN Internal Justice System

Since the UN internal justice system is only accessible to UN staff members, disputes involving consultants, contractors and UN volunteers have been settled through other means, including recourse to arbitration. Discussions about access to justice in the United Nations for these three categories are still underway as a dispute mechanism is being considered under a newly revised administrative issuance.

According to the SG's 2022 Report: *"(...) the new dispute settlement procedure will include a phase comprising strengthened informal amicable dispute resolution and, if that fails, procedures for a streamlined and simplified expedited arbitration to be adjudicated by a sole arbitrator based on the recently adopted expedited arbitration rules of the United Nations Commission on International Trade Law (UNCITRAL) with effect on 19 September 2021 (see A/76/17, A/77/156, 26/68 22-11017 para 189)."*

According to the report, the new dispute settlement procedures for consultants and individual contractors will facilitate dispute settlement by making the process less costly and time-consuming for both non-staff personnel and the United Nations.

The report states the Secretary-General is examining the cost-effective engagement of a neutral entity that would support such ad hoc arbitration proceedings by appointing sole arbitrators and providing registry services. For that purpose, it has identified the Permanent Court of Arbitration as well-placed to provide such support.

The Permanent Court of Arbitration is an intergovernmental organisation established by treaty in 1899 and, so far, it has been the only arbitration institution dedicated exclusively to the administration of disputes involving various combinations of States, State-owned entities, intergovernmental organisations and private individuals.

The Permanent Court of Arbitration would support the conduct of arbitration proceedings between the United Nations and non-staff personnel under the UNCITRAL Expedited Arbitration Rules for an all-inclusive fee of 3000 euros *per* case. This fee would be covered by the United Nations office where the dispute with the non-staff personnel arises, while the arbitrator's fees and costs would be shared equally between the parties pending the allocation of costs in the arbitral award.

The overall idea is that the Court's support would include appointing a sole arbitrator and providing administrative and registry services to the parties and the arbitrator during the arbitration.

The primary purpose of the Court's support would be to reduce the costs that would otherwise be incurred by the sole arbitrator carrying out administrative tasks, including maintaining an archive of filings and correspondence, holding and disbursing the arbitration deposits, organising hearings and meetings between the sole arbitrator and the parties, offering general secretarial or linguistic support, and any other tasks entrusted to it by the arbitrator or the parties.

We fail to understand why these three categories of individuals were kept outside the internal justice system and the UN has opted for an alternative model of dispute resolution.

From our point of view, to include vendors and consultants in the UNDT statute and allow them to pursue their grievances in the internal justice system would contribute to a more uniform treatment of these individuals, would significantly reduce costs for themselves (as access to the UNDT is free of charge and in most cases, OSLA represents the complainant) with minimal impact on the organisation's activities and business needs.

7 Legal Standing and the Role of Staff Associations

The words Staff Association or Staff Union refer essentially to the same reality: "in essence, a voluntary association of employees and/or others in a relationship pursuant to which they perform services by way of personal exertion, who have agreed together to act collectively through that association or union to protect and promote their industrial interests."[10]

In the context of the United Nations common system, there have always been both staff associations and staff unions that have similar aims and carry out similar functions on behalf of their members. Some believe that the use of the name "staff association" reflects the professional nature of the work of international civil servants and projects a gentler and more accommodating image, whereas others believe that using the name "staff union" lends an image associated with militarism and an adversarial relationship.[11]

Therefore, the role played by staff associations in international organisations goes far beyond legal standing, access to tribunals and internal appeal mechanisms. Indeed, staff associations are an intrinsic part of policy-making in international organisations while ensuring a balance and an appropriate level playing field for international civil servants in negotiations with senior management related to their employment, by acting as a "pressure group."

In contrast to trade unions, international staff associations or unions have a built-in limitation: their statutory loyalty to the organisation. As international civil servants, staff representatives are committed to accepting and promoting the

[10] See ILOAT Judgement 2672.

[11] See 18–06105 E-BRO FICSA Handbook, consulted online on 23 July 2024 at https://ficsa.org/fileadmin/user_upload/18-06105E_BRO_FICSA_Handbook_WEB.pdf.

objectives of their organisation, discharging their international functions and regulating their conduct with the interests of the organisation alone in view.[12]

Apart from *amicus curiae* provisions in the UNDT statute (Article 24) and two other provisions enshrined in the Statute of the Administrative Tribunal of the Francophonie and the OECD Administrative Tribunal, there are barely any provisions on the legal standing of staff associations in the statutes of other international administrative tribunals or appeal bodies.

Nonetheless, Petrovic (former Registrar of the ILOAT) points out that the case law of some tribunals has recognised the right of staff representatives to invoke certain rights conferred on staff unions (such as the right to be consulted, to have facilities accorded to them, or to the freedom of communication with their members) as individual rights within the framework of the freedom of association.

In his view, this pragmatic approach is not satisfactory and legal standing should be granted to a certain extent to staff associations.[13]

An overview of the jurisprudence of the ILOAT will allow a clearer perspective of the problem at stake.

In 1996, a ILOAT judgement involving *Eurocontrol* specifically addressed the issue of whether a complainant may rely on a collective agreement between an organisation and its staff.[14]

From the Tribunal's perspective, "(. . .) it is a truth universally acknowledged that the collective agreement is a basic vehicle of social progress, justice and peace. That that is so, is due to the International Labour Organization, among others, and to its international instruments such as the right to organise and Collective Bargaining Convention, 1949 (No. 98), and the Labour Relations (public service) Convention, 1978 (No. 151)."

In another judgement,[15] the same tribunal clarified that a collective agreement becomes an intrinsic part of the internal law of an international organisation once it is accepted by it:

> An international organisation is free to choose whatever methods or means it likes—be they formal rules or contracts of employment—to define the terms of appointment of staff. But any collective agreement it does conclude becomes part of the law of the international civil service. Signing such an agreement puts it under obligations in law; a member of its staff may plead such obligations in a complaint to the Tribunal; and the Tribunal will review compliance with the letter and spirit of the agreement.

[12] Idem.

[13] See Petrovic (n.d.), pp. 59–76.

[14] See ILOAT Judgement 1369 (1994, 77th session).

[15] ILOAT Judgement 1311, accessed on 23 July 2023 at https://webapps.ilo.org/dyn/triblex/triblexmain.detail?p_lang=en&p_judgment_no=1311&p_keyword_id=609&p_language_code=EN

This jurisprudence is pioneering and innovative in the context of international administrative law, as it brings into the internal legal systems of international organisations elements of labour law which are somehow extraneous to this context.

In general, international organisations are reluctant to recognise staff unions or staff associations a legal right to contest internal decisions on behalf of their associates and, in most cases, there are no collective agreements in these organisations.

In most cases, staff unions' interventions are limited to ad hoc negotiations with senior management when new policies, review of older policies or restructuring exercises are to be put in place.

Contrary to what happens in continental Europe, in which staff unions and staff associations can represent their associates in legal actions before national courts, international organisations do not contemplate said prerogatives in their internal frameworks neither at an individual nor a collective level.

In WHO, for example, the Global Staff Management Council (GSMC) is the principal consultative body which brings together management and staff associations annually to discuss personnel policies and service conditions, but it has no executive nor legislative powers.

International organisations fear that granting legal standing to staff unions will increase internal litigation, prevent, or obstruct the implementation of new policies and, ultimately, paralyse their operational needs and affect their overall mandate.

The underlying reasons for this are anchored in the prevailing managerial culture in international organisations, as top officials and senior managers tend to feel reluctant to engage in negotiations with staff representatives who they perceive as a limitation to their managerial discretion.

Therefore, the role of staff associations limits itself to the consultation stage of policy-making procedures. Staff associations do not have legal standing before internal tribunals or appeal bodies and their intervention in legal proceedings is normally limited to "friends of the court."

8 Staff Associations as *Amicus Curiae* in Judicial Proceedings

Throughout a seven-year mandate as a judge in the UNDT, I have experienced only one request for intervention as *amicus curiae* from UNHCR's staff association in relation to the implementation of a UNHCR policy[16] which has never been previously "judicially tested."

In the UNHCR case, the Staff Council pointed out that the Tribunal's decision "will have a significant impact on a large number of staff members in UNHCR" who are currently in between assignments or who will be in between assignments in the future.[17]

---

[16] Internally known as SIBA policy.

[17] This reasoning is expressed in Order No. 006/GVA/ 2020 issued in case UNDT/GVA/2019/069, which is available online at https://www.un.org/internaljustice/oaj/en. Accessed on 23 July 2024.

In its request for participation as *amicus curiae,* the Staff Council indicated that it had raised its concerns regarding the legality of UNHCR's newly introduced SLWOP[18] within SIBA[19] in numerous occasions before and after its adoption.

Staff Council further mentioned that it sought to share with the Tribunal "its knowledge of the issues at hand and their impact on staff." In addition, the Staff Council indicated that it would provide the Tribunal with "some background information on the SIBA phenomenon, its scale and some of the reasons for its continued existence."

The Tribunal considered that the Staff Council should be allowed to intervene as a *friend-of-the-court* in the case, under Art. 24 of the Tribunal's Rules of Procedure as its participation would assist the Tribunal in its deliberations.

In fact, under Article 24 of the UNDT's Rules of Procedure:

1. A staff association may submit a signed application to file a friend-of the court brief on a form to be prescribed by the Registrar, which may be transmitted electronically. The Registrar shall forward a copy of the application to the parties, who shall have three days to file any objections, which shall be submitted on a prescribed form.
2. The President or the judge hearing the case may grant the application if it considers that the filling of the brief would assist the Dispute Tribunal in its deliberations. The decision will be communicated to the applicant and the parties by the Registrar.

In the present case, the Tribunal was to examine, for the first time, the legality of the UNHCR's newly introduced measure of placing staff members in between assignments ("SIBA") on SLWOP.

The Tribunal admitted participation of the staff association, bearing in mind the important contribution that the Staff Council could provide in relation to the reasons that led to introducing SLWOP within the SIBA mechanism, as well as, to the procedure that was followed for its implementation. The Tribunal considered that the Staff Council could also provide relevant information concerning the impact of said policy on UNHCR staff at large.

Nonetheless, the Tribunal reminded UNHCR Staff Council that the role of a *friend-of-the-court* was different from the role played by the parties.

In fact, *friends-of-the-court* could not directly intervene in case management discussion(s) or at the hearing even though they could be present. Furthermore, *friends-of-the-court* could neither examine nor cross-examine witnesses and did not have the right to appeal.

In the above-mentioned case, *friends-of-the-court's* intervention was limited to filing submissions on legal issues of a complex nature related to the newly introduced measure(s) of placing SIBA staff members on SLWOP.

Despite statutory limitations to the role of staff associations, their intervention in court proceedings is neither irrelevant nor innocuous. In fact, staff associations are in

[18] SLWOP is the acronym for Special Leave Without Pay.

[19] SIBA is a specific policy implemented in UNHCR that regulates placement of staff members between assignments.

general better positioned to convey to the tribunal the underlying reasons that justify the implementation of a given policy, to assess its impact on staff members and to evaluate and monitor how it will evolve over time.

On the other hand, their participation in judicial proceedings has a political dimension which cannot be overlooked either by the tribunals or the administration.

International organisations fear the impact of said judicial intervention and its consequences on the balance of forces between staff and managers.

From my perspective, the current *status quo* is a consequence of member states and senior management fearing collateral phenomena of judicial activism and staff over-empowerment.

Nonetheless, transparency and public accountability would demand a strengthening of the role played by staff representatives in the managerial affairs of international organisations.

9 Conclusion

Locus standi is a *conditio sine qua non* of access to internal justice systems of international organisations and its importance goes far beyond a procedural requirement, as it reflects the existing level playing field of internal justice systems.

In general, access to those justice systems is an exclusive prerogative of staff members. Consultants, experts and interns do not have legal standing before internal tribunals, and several ad hoc solutions have been put in place, by different organisations, to solve conflicts between the organisation and external hires.

Another interesting feature of those internal justice systems is that almost none of the contemporary IOs (being those of a financial or a humanitarian nature) grant legal access to its tribunals or boards of appeal to staff associations.

Similarly, none admit judicial review of regulatory decisions or "collective actions."

This is a situation which is likely to persist in the coming years.

From our perspective, the underlying reasons for this *status quo* relate to political reluctance to allow staff associations or staff unions to influence policies and decision-making processes of IOs and it is intended to prevent strengthening staff members' positions vis-a-vis the administration.

On the other hand, managers and state members do not want to grant judicial organs a way to limit managerial discretion and to determine how IOs exercise their mandate.

Nonetheless, staff associations can still play an essential role in the workplace. Indeed, they may become active stakeholders in negotiations with senior management, provide legal assistance to their associates, dynamise trainings, be directly involved in initiatives related to the prevention of harassment and monitor the overall work environment and the well-being of their associates.

Jurisprudence

United Nations Appeals Tribunal
- 2015-UNAT-526
- 2017-UNAT-750
- 2015-UNAT-563
- 2011-UNAT-171
- 2011-UNAT-148
- 2011-UNAT-139
- 2022-UNAT-1262
- 2017-UNAT-758
- 2003-UNAT-1157

United Nations Dispute Tribunal
- UNDT/GVA/2015/118
- UNDT/GVA/2019/069
- UNDT/GVA/2021/089

International Labour Organisation Administrative Tribunal
- Judgement No. 2672
- Judgement No. 1369
- Judgement No. 1311

Electronic Resources

- https://www.un.org/internaljustice/oaj/en
- https://ficsa.org/fileadmin/user_upload/1806105E_BRO_FICSA_Handbook_WEB.pdf
- https://ilostaffunion.org/en/areas-of-action/international-relations-representations
- https://www.ilo.org/dyn/triblex/triblexmain.showList?p_lang=en
- https://www.un.org/en/ga/sixth/77/admin_of_justice.shtml

Reference

Petrovic, D. (n.d.). Access to Justice - An unfinished task. In *International administrative justice and international organisations: Overview and prospects* (pp. 59–76). International Colloquy, ADB Group.

Harassment Investigations in International Organizations: Rights of Claimants under the Jurisprudence of the International Labour Organization Administrative Tribunal (ILOAT)

Ruth Szabó

Contents

1 Introduction 53
2 Defining Workplace Harassment 55
3 Internal Investigations 59
4 Scope of Judicial Review in Harassment Cases 60
4.1 General Principles in Harassment Cases 61
4.2 Judicial Review in Harassment Investigations 63
5 Due Process in Harassment Investigations 67
5.1 Claimants' Rights to "Test" the Evidence and Be Given an Opportunity to Prove Their Allegations 68
5.2 Claimants' Rights in Relation to Witnesses 71
6 Conclusion 72
References 73

1 Introduction

Harassment in the workplace is not a new issue for international organizations. Still, in recent years the number of complaints from employees claiming they are a victim of harassment, including sexual harassment, has significantly increased. As employers of a diverse and mobile workforce, international organizations are obligated to maintain a healthy work environment free from all forms of harassment

Ruth Szabó, legal consultant to international organizations on employee relations and internal dispute resolution, and former lawyer at the United Nations Secretariat, the World Health Organization and Gavi, the Vaccine Alliance (www.ruthszabo.com).

R. Szabó (✉)
Independent Lawyer, Investigator and Mediator, London, UK

T. Bravo, K. Bradley (eds.), *Judicial Review in International Administrative Law*, Law for Professionals, https://doi.org/10.1007/978-3-031-71840-3_4

and other improper workplace behaviors (collectively, "workplace harassment").[1] Consequently, international organizations have adopted policies that articulate ethical values and standards of behavior, and the consequences of breaches thereof. They are also encouraging the early resolution of employee conflicts through alternative dispute resolution mechanisms, such as mediation, and have established the resources and processes to investigate allegations of workplace harassment and, if warranted, to impose disciplinary measures on wrongdoers.

In the past, internal investigations into employee misconduct focused on the procedural safeguards of the alleged offenders, and appeals to international administrative tribunals were mostly brought by them in the context of challenging a disciplinary measure. More recently, the victims of workplace harassment are increasingly challenging the decisions of executive heads when their harassment claims are not accepted by the organization. Consequently, the various international administrative tribunals established to hear and adjudicate employment disputes between international organizations and their employees have been shaping the legal principles that underpin the handling of allegations of workplace harassment also from the perspective of the claimants. This is particularly so of the International Labour Organization Administrative Tribunal ("ILOAT" or the "Tribunal"), the oldest judicial body amongst the various international administrative tribunals established to adjudicate employment disputes between international civil servants and their employer, with currently some fifty-eight international organizations under its jurisdiction.[2]

[1]For this chapter, "workplace" refers to any physical location, including outside office premises, and under any circumstances, used for the purposes of, or otherwise associated with, or having an impact on, the individual's work.

[2]The Administrative Tribunal of the International Labour Organization was established on 9 October 1946, replacing the Administrative Tribunal of the League of Nations (established in 1927). With the winding up of the League of Nations, its administrative tribunal was transferred to the International Labour Organization (ILO) when the ILO became a specialized agency of the United Nations. The Tribunal is competent to hear staff complaints against other inter-governmental organizations provided the organization recognized the Tribunal's jurisdiction and met certain criteria specified in the Tribunal's Statute. Since 1998, international entities that are not strictly or exclusively inter-governmental have also been permitted to become parties to the Tribunal provided they similarly meet certain conditions (see ILOAT Statute and Rules, Edition 2021). The Tribunal has jurisdiction over complaints alleging non-observance (in substance or in form) of the terms of appointment of officials and of provisions of staff regulations of international organizations that recognize the jurisdiction of the Tribunal. If satisfied that the complaint is well founded, the Tribunal may order the rescinding of the decision impugned or the performance of the obligation relied upon, or, alternatively, award compensation to the complainant for injury. ILOAT judgments are final and without appeal. According to the Tribunal's website (https://www.ilo.org/tribunal/lang%2D%2Den/index.htm), to date, the ILOAT has adopted more than 4700 judgments and is open to more than 58,000 current or former international civil servants from 58 organizations under its jurisdiction. These organizations include the majority of the UN Specialized Agencies such as the International Organization for Migration (IOM), the World Health Organization (WHO), the Food and Agriculture Organization (FAO), the International Telecommunications Union (ITU), the International Labour Organization (ILO), United Nations Educational, Scientific and Cultural Organization (UNESCO), the United Nations Industrial Development Organization (UNIDO), the

International organizations have recently had their fair share of media attention concerning improper behavior in the workplace, particularly when the perpetrators are senior officials. The focus has principally been on allegations of sexual exploitation and abuse in local communities in field operations, although the press has also reported on cases of sexual harassment and other wrongdoings in the workplace.[3] Organizations are responding by increasing harassment awareness and prevention training, reinforcing "zero tolerance" policies, and bolstering their internal investigative capacity. In today's world, efficient and robust investigations are essential to guard against reputational risks and to ensure safe workplaces for employees. In this context, the jurisprudence of the ILOAT provides guidance to international organizations—particularly those under its jurisdiction—in their handling of internal investigations into allegations of workplace harassment, including on the balancing of the respective interests of those involved.

This chapter explores the evolving jurisprudence of the ILOAT relevant to the conduct of harassment investigations. It focuses on key judgments that bear on the rights of employees who allege they are the victims of workplace harassment (hereinafter "claimants"). Specifically, I discuss the challenges to international organizations and their investigative functions of developments in the ILOAT's case law pertaining to due process rights of claimants and consider whether there is coherent judicial precedent in this area providing clear guidance to international organizations and their employees.

2 Defining Workplace Harassment

There is no single definition of workplace harassment across all international organizations, but the concept is generally understood to mean improper and unwelcome actions or behaviors, whether of a verbal, non-verbal, or physical nature,

World Intellectual Property Organization (WIPO), other organizations that also apply the UN common system, such the International Atomic Energy Agency (IAEA) or the Preparatory Committee for the Comprehensive Nuclear-Test-Ban Treaty Organization (CTBTO), several regional organizations such as the European Patent Office (EPO), the European Organization for the Safety of Air Navigation (Eurocontrol) to "hybrid" organizations such as the International Federation of Red Cross and Red Crescent Societies or the Global Fund to fight AIDS, Tuberculosis and Malaria (Global Fund), to name just a few.

[3]For example, press reports of sexual harassment at UNAIDS (2018/2019) that led to the "Report by an Independent Expert Panel on Prevention and Response to Harassment, including sexual harassment, bullying and abuse of power at UNAIDS Secretariat" (UNAIDS /PCB (43)/CRP1). Other examples are press reports on complaints of harassment, abuse of authority and discrimination at the World Food Programme (2019); press reports on allegations of sexual exploitation and abuse by WHO officials in the Democratic Republic of Congo, leading to the establishment and Report of the Independent Commission to review the allegations (*The New Humanitarian and Thomson Reuter Foundation*, 29 September 2020: "Exclusive: More than 50 women accuse aid workers of sex abuse in Congo Ebola crisis." See also UK British Broadcasting Corporation (BBC) Documentary entitled "The Whistleblowers: Inside the UN," June 2022.

perpetrated by superiors or colleagues against another or others, that unreasonably interfere with work or create a hostile work environment.[4]

International organizations normally refer in their internal rules to different forms that workplace harassment can take, including "psychological harassment" and "bullying/mobbing" which normally involve repeated offensive, humiliating, aggressive, or intimidating behavior having the cumulative effect of undermining or demeaning another, and "sexual harassment" which can range from inappropriate remarks of a sexual nature to *quid pro quo* abuse of authority. Workplace harassment can also manifest itself in the form of acts of discrimination and retaliation, although the act of "retaliation" is more typically associated with, and regulated by, policies aimed at encouraging the reporting of alleged wrongdoings and protecting whistle-blowers. Other than sexual harassment, which in some international organizations is the object of a specific definition, as well as preventative, investigative, and remedial mechanisms,[5] workplace harassment in most international organizations covers a wide range of behaviors varying from inter-relational frictions between co-workers to acts of sexual assault and discrimination that in some national legal systems would amount to criminal offenses.

Organizations will generally include in their internal rules the possibility that one serious incident would suffice for a finding of misconduct based on harassment.[6] In practice, except where that one incident can reasonably be said to amount to sexual misconduct or an abuse of authority, workplace harassment normally involves a pattern of detrimental actions and behaviors perpetuated over time. According to the

[4]The Standards of Conduct for the International Civil Service (2013) adopted by the International Civil Service Commission which is binding on the UN common system organizations provides that:

"21. Harassment in any shape or form is an affront to human dignity and international civil servants must not engage in any form of harassment. International civil servants have the right to a workplace environment free of harassment or abuse. All organizations must prohibit any kind of harassment. Organizations have a duty to establish rules and provide guidance on what constitutes harassment and abuse of authority and how unacceptable behaviour will be addressed.

22. International civil servants must not abuse their authority or use their power or position in a manner that is offensive, humiliating or embarrassing to another person."

[5]In 2018, the United Nations System Chief Executives Board for Coordination endorsed a UN System Model Policy on Sexual Harassment on the recommendation of the Board's High-level Committee on Management. The model policy was developed by the CEB Task Force on Addressing Sexual Harassment within the Organizations of the UN System. The model policy provides for a uniform definition of "sexual harassment" as "any unwelcome conduct of a sexual nature that might reasonably be expected or be perceived to cause offense or humiliation, when such conduct interferes with work, is made a condition of employment or creates an intimidating, hostile or offensive work environment. Sexual harassment may occur in the workplace or in connection with work. While typically involving a pattern of conduct, sexual harassment may take the form of a single incident. In assessing the reasonableness of expectations or perceptions, the perspective of the person who is the target of the conduct shall be considered." This definition is often used in the policies of other international organizations.

[6]This has also been confirmed in the jurisprudence—see, for example, ILOAT Judgment No. 2594 (2007) *P. v. WIPO*, consideration 18. Additionally, UNAT Judgment No. 2010-UNAT-012 (Parker) para 38.

ILOAT's case law, workplace harassment should be determined in light of the behavior itself and the effects of such behavior on the individual(s) concerned.[7] It is the perception that the person who is the target of the behavior "*may reasonably and objectively have of acts or remarks liable to demean or humiliate him/her.*"[8] Moreover, under the Tribunal's case law harassing behaviors can be deliberate or unconscious. In other words, actions or behaviors may constitute harassment even where there is no intent on the part of the perpetrator to offend or intimidate, humiliate, or otherwise mistreat the other(s).[9] The ILOAT also considers as harassment the result of the cumulative effect of several incidents, which, taken in isolation, might not in and of themselves be viewed as harassment.[10]

Yet, not all actions or behaviors that are perceived by an individual as harassment will necessarily constitute harassment. The normal exercise of supervisory responsibility and the provision of negative feedback intended to be constructive in the context of performance appraisals would not normally be regarded as constituting harassment. To the ILOAT, actions or behaviors that can be said to constitute harassment are those for which there are no reasonable explanations.[11] In other words, managerially reasonable actions would not constitute harassment unless there is evidence of ill will or prejudice[12] or if the actions are carried out in a manner that a

[7] See, for example, ILOAT Judgment No. 3400 (2015) *A. v. FAO*, consideration 7, wherein the Tribunal held by reference to the Organization's definition of harassment that: "Whether behaviour is improper or not depends on the content of the behaviour, not intention. At least ordinarily, whether the behaviour is directed at and whether it is offensive to another person does not, again, depend on intention or at least an intention to harass."

[8] See ILOAT Judgment No. 4265 (2020) *L. (No. 5) v. EPO*, consideration 6.

[9] See, for example, ILOAT Judgment No. 4207 (2020) *G.M. v. IAEA*, consideration 20: "It is noted that the Tribunal has specifically rejected the assumption that intent on the part of the alleged perpetrator is required in order to establish harassment (see, for example, Judgments 2524, consideration 25; 3233, consideration 6; and 3692, consideration 18, and the case law cited therein)."

[10] See, for example, ILOAT Judgment No. 4253 (2020) *Z. v. ILO*, consideration 5. Citing earlier case law, the Tribunal stated: "Indeed, harassment may involve a series of acts over time (see Judgments 2067, consideration 16, and 4034 consideration 16) and can be the result of the cumulative effect of several manifestations of conduct which, taken in isolation, might not be viewed as harassment (see, for example, Judgments 3485, consideration 6 and 3599, consideration 4), even if they were not challenged at the time when they occurred (see, for example, Judgment 3841, consideration 6)."

[11] See, for example, ILOAT Judgment No. 4038 (2018) *G. v. ILO*, consideration 18 (citing Judgments 3447, consideration 9 and 2524, consideration 25.)

[12] See ILOAT Judgment No. 2524 (2006) *F.V. v. CTBTO*, consideration 25: "[...] behaviour will not be characterized as harassment or mobbing if there is a reasonable explanation for the conduct in question (see Judgment 2370, under 17. On the other hand, an explanation which is prima facie reasonable may be rejected if there is evidence of ill will or prejudice or if the behaviour in question is disproportionate to the matter which is said to have prompted the course taken."

manager ought to have known would have offended or humiliated the individual concerned notwithstanding being managerially reasonable.[13]

An additional category of harassment that is not typically defined in the personnel policies of international organizations but which the ILOAT expects organizations to consider when interpreting their internal rules is that of "institutional harassment."[14] According to the ILOAT's former Registrar, Dražen Petrović, international organizations ought not to consider harassment as "*exclusively an inter-personal problem.*"[15] Petrović notes that institutional harassment occurs when it is difficult to identify one single person or one single incident that causes prejudice to an official.[16] The Tribunal describes it as a series of acts of mismanagement or omissions by the organization for which there is no reasonable explanation, that deeply and adversely affect the dignity and career objectives of the individual concerned.[17] Institutional harassment is a relatively new concept and generally less well understood. It has created new challenges for organizations whose investigative bodies will be expected to address allegations of institutional harassment within their mandate,[18] notwithstanding that the actions complained of are typically administrative decisions normally contested by employees before the organizations' internal justice mechanism.

[13] In ILOAT Judgment No. 4241 (2020) *N. (No. 2) v. WHO/UNAIDS*, at consideration 19, the Tribunal found that certain actions considered by the investigative function to have been consistent with the perpetrator's managerial function did nonetheless amount to harassment. This was because the perpetrator held senior management roles in international organizations and a leading role in the performance management system at the organization in question and therefore ought reasonably to have known that the action (of delegating to a junior official in her office some of her supervisory duties over the complainant) would have offended and humiliated the complainant.

[14] See ILOAT Judgment No. 4378 (2021), *T. v. WHO*, consideration 4. The Tribunal noted that a complaint of harassment against a department (in this case the WHO's Internal Oversight Office) had to be investigated as it could amount to institutional harassment. See also ILOAT Judgment No. 3250 (2014) *L.N. v. ILO*, consideration 9, where the Tribunal qualified a cumulative series of detrimental administrative actions which "deeply and adversely affected the complainant's dignity and career objectives" as "institutional harassment."

[15] Petrović (2021), p. 186.

[16] Ibid., p. 187.

[17] See, for example, ILOAT Judgment No. 4345 (2020) *R. (No. 4) v. IAEA*, consideration 8. See also ILOAT Judgment No. 4111 (2019) *V.B. v. ILO*, consideration 7 citing Judgment No. 3250 (2014) *L. N. v. ILO*, consideration 1 wherein the Tribunal defined institutional harassment as "vertical top-down harassment" and at consideration 9: "*in this case [...] it is the accumulation of repeated events which deeply and adversely affected the complainant's dignity and career objectives...[T]he Tribunal is of the opinion that this administrative wrongdoing can be defined as institutional harassment.*"

[18] As noted by the ILOAT in Judgment No. 4344 (2020) *A. (No. 2) v. IAEA*, consideration 6: "*a finding that a staff member was subjected to any form of harassment, including institutional harassment, is first within the investigative purview of OIOS upon a report of harassment made to it.*"

3 Internal Investigations

The internal investigation into allegations of employee misconduct is one tool to help organizations ensure a safe workplace and protect their employees. In the past, investigations into employee misconduct were carried out largely by auditors. Now organizations are engaging specialist investigators either as part of their oversight/audit teams or on an ad hoc basis. Investigators gather all the relevant facts and draw conclusions on the sufficiency of the evidence, determining whether the allegations are substantiated. Investigators may conclude that there is a basis for initiating disciplinary proceedings but are not the decision-makers on whether this happens. Nonetheless, the internal investigation is central to an effective and fair disciplinary process and largely serves as the basis for any subsequent administrative decisions, including disciplinary sanctions, affecting the individual(s) concerned. The investigation report and the underlying process on which it is based are therefore open to judicial review and scrutiny.

Many international organizations have established an internal investigative function[19] and/or have formalized their investigation practices and procedures in guidelines or manuals which typically form part of the employment framework and are made available to their personnel. These protocols set out the different stages and consequences of the investigation process, from the preliminary assessment of the allegations (which forms the basis for deciding whether an investigation is warranted) to the fact-finding investigation, including the principles and methodologies for interviewing and gathering material facts and evidence, whether inculpatory or exculpatory, and the due process considerations.

Notwithstanding the written guidance, investigations into allegations of harassment are rarely straightforward. They are intrusive to the parties, can exacerbate an already negative working relationship, and often impact the wider working environment, particularly as colleagues may feel they are being asked to take sides in an interpersonal dispute or to "snitch" on their co-workers. These cases are complex, involving an analysis of individual behaviors, personalities, and conflictual relationships, and are mostly reliant on witness testimonies as the only source of evidentiary material. Situations are rarely clear-cut. The line between poor management practices and harassment is not always obvious. Investigators may need to determine the point at which an act of mismanagement becomes harassment,[20] and

[19]See the Report of the Joint Inspection Unit (2020): "Review of the state of the investigation function: progress made in the United Nations system organizations in strengthening the investigation function"; JIU/REP/2020/1. The review noted that despite the progress made over the past decade by international organizations that have established and professionalized their investigative function, organizations continue to face challenges, including because of the significant increase in caseload and the added complexities and difficulties associated with investigating allegations involving interpersonal behaviors, particularly sexual misconduct.

[20]The ILOAT has, for example, overruled investigators who have found that certain behaviors amounted to mismanagement and not harassment. See, for example, ILOAT Judgment No. 3318 (2014) *E.D.G. v. FAO,* consideration 8—the Investigative Panel had concluded that this was a case

assess the credibility of the parties where opposing views are expressed by witnesses.

Moreover, investigators may face witnesses who are reluctant to participate in the process despite the legal duty of employees of international organizations to cooperate with investigations. Witness reluctance can be partially addressed by reference to the protection against retaliation provided for in the internal rules of international organizations. In practice, however, this argument is often insufficient to assuage the concerns of witnesses about the possible negative impacts to them. Additionally, investigators can no longer provide witnesses with assurances that their names and testimony will not be shared with the parties to the harassment complaint in light of the ILOAT's broad interpretation of the *audi alteram partem* principle, as reflected in its more recent case law discussed below (in sect. 5).

4 Scope of Judicial Review in Harassment Cases

It is not within the purview of international administrative tribunals to conduct harassment investigations. The ILOAT has consistently stated that its scope of judicial review in harassment cases is not to reweigh the evidence, and that deference must be accorded to the investigative body that has had the benefit of hearing the persons involved and assessing their credibility. Where an investigative body has heard evidence and made findings of fact based on its appreciation of that evidence, the Tribunal's review is limited to assessing whether a manifest error of judgment has occurred.[21]

Notwithstanding the limited scope of judicial review on the findings of fact, the ILOAT often sets aside the discretionary decisions of executive heads of international organizations on account of procedural flaws in the conduct of the investigation. This is because of non-compliance with internal procedures or, more typically, with general principles of law (i.e., due process).[22] This is seemingly so irrespective of whether the procedural flaw is sufficiently substantial and prejudicial to dislodge a finding of misconduct that is borne out by the facts.[23]

of "shortcomings" in management and supervision, but the ILOAT concluded that it was a case of harassment as defined under the Organization's policy.

[21] See, for example, ILOAT Judgment No. 4579 (2022) *M. v. Global Fund to Fight AIDS, Tuberculosis and Malaria*, consideration 4; ILOAT Judgment No. 4279 (2020) *A. M. (No. 5) v. Eurocontrol*, consideration 7; ILOAT Judgment 3593 (2016) *E. v. FAO*, consideration 12.

[22] The ILOAT assesses each case on the basis of the rules of the organization concerned—see Article II(1) of the Statute and Rules of the Tribunal (available on the Tribunal's website see *supra.* Footnote 5). However, while not expressly indicated in its Statute, the Tribunal also refers in its reasoning of cases to "general principles of law."

[23] See, for example, ILOAT Judgment No. 4579 (2022) *M. v. Global Fund to Fight AIDS, Tuberculosis and Malaria*. In this case, the Tribunal set aside the decision of the Organization to dismiss the complaint for sexual harassment on the grounds that the individual had been charged with a lesser offense (misconduct) but sanctioned for the higher offense of gross misconduct. The UNAT takes a different approach in that under its "consistent jurisprudence only substantial

4.1 General Principles in Harassment Cases

The ILOAT has been shaping the legal principles and due process safeguards that it considers ought to govern the handling of harassment allegations. Several such principles are found in the common international jurisprudence of the ILOAT and the United Nations Appeals Tribunal (UNAT).[24] For example, both tribunals recognize that international organizations have a duty to provide a safe work environment free from harassment,[25] and therefore an obligation, when harassment allegations are made, to act on the complaint by initiating an investigation (at least a preliminary assessment of the allegations).[26] The investigation must be conducted objectively,

---

procedural irregularities will render a disciplinary measure unlawful. Even a very severe disciplinary measure like separation from service can be regarded as lawful if, despite some procedural irregularities, there is clear and convincing evidence of grave misconduct." UNAT Judgment 2018-UNAT-889, (Sall), para 33.

[24] In 2009, the United Nations Secretariat introduced major reforms to its internal justice system. The former United Nations Administrative Tribunal was abolished and replaced by a two-tiered judicial system, consisting of three Dispute Tribunals that would hear cases in the first instance and one Appeals Tribunal. Both staff members and the Secretary-General may appeal decisions of the Dispute Tribunals (UNDT) to the Appeals Tribunal (UNAT).

[25] See, for example, ILOAT Judgment No. 4344 (2020) *A. (No. 2) v. IAEA*, consideration 3: "Regarding an organization's duties where harassment complaints are made, the Tribunal has stated, for example in Judgment 4207, consideration 15, that an international organization has a duty to provide a safe and adequate working environment for its staff members and that given the serious nature of a claim of harassment, an organization has an obligation to initiate the investigation itself." Additionally, ILOAT Judgment No. 4171 (2019) F. (Nos. 5, 6, and 7 v. UNESCO, consideration 11, where the Tribunal held: "In its case law, the Tribunal has emphasised that the relations between an international organisation and its staff members must be governed by good faith, respect, transparency and consideration for their dignity (see Judgment 1479, consideration 12). An organisation must therefore treat its staff with proper consideration and avoid causing them undue injury. It must care for the dignity of its staff members and not cause them unnecessary personal distress and disappointment where this could be avoided (see, for example, Judgments 1756, consideration 10(a), and 3353, consideration 26). As the Tribunal held in Judgment 2524, an international organisation has a duty to provide a safe and adequate environment for its staff (see also Judgment 2706, consideration 5)." See also UNAT Judgment No. 2014-UNAT-409 (Nogueira), para 18, wherein the UNAT confirmed that the Appellant was "entitled to an effective remedy for the violation of his legal rights to a workplace free of any form of harassment." Additionally, see UNAT Judgment 2019-UNAT-939 (Delaunay), wherein the UNAT reaffirmed that an organization has a duty to protect its staff from harassment, the failure of which may lead to an award of damages.

[26] In ILOAT Judgment No. 1619 (1997) *In re Eben-Moussi, WHO*, at consideration 6, the Tribunal ruled that "[w]hen a staff member makes charges as serious as sexual harassment an organisation must do its utmost to afford protection. But it must at the same time carry out a full and proper inquiry that respects the rights of the accused." Even earlier in ILOAT Judgment No. 1340 (1994) *In re Vollering (No. 3), EPO*, at consideration 14, the Tribunal held: "subordinates are vulnerable to criticism by superiors and if criticism is untrue must be protected from unjust attack. In this case, there was a duty on the Organization to make an investigation. Since it failed to take any such action the complainant is awarded moral damages for its failure to protect and vindicate his good name." See, more recently, for example, ILOAT Judgment 4233 (2020) *C. d. L. (No. 2) v. OIE*, consideration 2, wherein the Tribunal held: "It is well established that an international organisation has a

thoroughly, efficiently and fairly.[27] Upon the conclusion of the investigation, the claimant is entitled to a response from the organization regarding the allegation of workplace harassment.[28] Where an injury occurs, the organization is obliged to assume liability towards the claimant.[29] This extends to protecting the claimant from any further harm[30] and awarding compensation for injury.[31] In relation to the

duty to its staff members to investigate claims of harassment thoroughly and objectively [. . .] The OIE is under such an obligation even though the existing rules do not provide for any specific procedure to deal with harassment complaints." See also UNAT Judgment No. 2010-UNAT-099 (Nwuke), paras 36–40, wherein the UNAT held that a staff member who alleges that they have been subjected to harassment may challenge a decision not to investigate their claim and overturning the UNDT's ruling that it could not compel the Organization to investigate the staff member's complaints of discrimination because the Appellant had not contested an "administrative decision that is alleged to be in non-compliance with the terms of [the Appellant's] appointment or contract of employment." In addition, UNAT Judgment 2017-UNAT-733 (Nadeau), paras 33–34, wherein UNAT held: "The Administration has a degree of discretion as to how to conduct a review and assessment of a complaint and whether to undertake an investigation regarding all or some of the allegations. Only in particular situations, i.e., in a case of a serious and reasonable accusation, *a staff member does have a right to an investigation against another staff member, and this process may be subject to judicial review*" (emphasis added).

[27] See, more generally, Waechter (2012), pp. 339–381.

[28] See ILOAT Judgment No. 4207 (2019) *G. M. v. IAEA*, consideration 15: "Upon the conclusion of the investigation, the complainant is entitled to a response from the Administration regarding the claim of harassment." See also ILOAT Judgment No. 4541 (2022) D. (No. 2) v. IFAD, consideration 4: "[. . .] the staff member who engaged the procedure, while not entitled to be informed of any measures taken against the alleged harasser, is entitled to a decision on the question of harassment itself [. . .] and, in consequence, to receive a reply from the administration concerning her or his harassment complaint."

[29] See ILOAT Judgment No. 4207 (2020) *G. M. v. IAEA*, consideration 15: "[. . .] as the Tribunal held in Judgment 2706, consideration 5, 'an international organisation is liable for all the injuries caused to a staff member by their supervisor acting in the course of his or her duties, when the victim is subjected to treatment that is an affront to his or her personal and professional dignity' (see also Judgments 1609, consideration 16, 1875, consideration 32, and 3170, consideration 33). Thus, an international organization must take proper actions to protect a victim of harassment." See also UNAT Judgment No. 2019-UNAT-939 (Delaunay): "The Organization has a duty to protect its staff from harassment. A failure to fulfil this duty may lead to an award of compensation." Additionally, UNAT Judgment No. 2014-UNAT-409 (Nogueira) para 16—the UNAT held: "[. . .] where there is a failure of the Administration to follow its own Rules and Regulations and that impacts and infringes the rights of a staff member, then as a general principle of law and the jurisprudence of this Tribunal, the staff member is entitled to an effective remedy."

[30] See, for example, ILOAT Judgment No. 4299 (2020) *R. (No. 6) v. IAEA*, consideration 5: "It is true that a staff member who has [. . .] established she or he has been harassed may also be entitled to an award of moral damages by the organization for the harassment (see, for example, Judgment 4158, consideration 3). Whether there is such an entitlement may depend on the terms of the regime in place within the organization to deal with harassment grievances. It is certainly something that can be awarded in proceedings in the Tribunal (see Judgment 4241, considerations 24 and 25). However, what is important is that, even if moral damages might be awarded, that is a subsidiary remedy or relief available in cases of this type when harassment is established. . .The primary obligation of the organization if harassment is proved is to protect the complainant and prevent further harassment."

[31] See ILOAT Judgment No. 4217 (2019) *L. v. IFAD*, at consideration 9, wherein the Tribunal set aside the decision of the Organization for refusal to grant a complainant of harassment

latter, the ILOAT's jurisprudence has recognized the general principle that it is the responsibility of the organization that establishes the existence of harassment to redress the injury caused and that, ordinarily, this redress should take the form of monetary compensation for the injury suffered.[32]

There is however no common position between the ILOAT and UNAT on the sharing of the investigation report with the claimant. The UNAT jurisprudence has it that the claimant of workplace harassment is entitled only to a summary account of the investigation findings and conclusions in accordance with the applicable UN regulation.[33] The ILOAT's case law appears to require the disclosure of the investigation report to the claimant after the organization has made its decision on the complaint, redacted if needed to protect the confidentiality of some elements of the process, so that the claimant may properly appeal the organization's decision on their complaint.[34]

4.2 Judicial Review in Harassment Investigations

On the conduct of the investigation, the ILOAT's consistent case law establishes that the process must be thorough and the facts must be determined objectively and in their overall context while not compromising the reputation of the alleged perpetrator.[35] At the same time, due process must be observed[36] and the investigation must

compensation for the injury caused in circumstances where the investigation report demonstrated she had been harassed. Other relevant ILOAT judgments include Judgment 4602 (2023) *F. v. WTO*, considerations 14 and 16, wherein the Tribunal stated that even in situations where there is no provision for compensation to victims of harassment in the internal regulations of the organization, its case law "clearly recognises the right to such compensation when properly supported."

[32] See ILOAT Judgment No. 4808 (2024) *G. v. ILO*, at consideration 11.

[33] See Judgment No: UNDT/2014/022 (Ivanov), para 25 and UNAT Judgment 2016-UNAT-662 (Masylkanova).

[34] See ILOAT Judgment No. 4541 (2022) *D. (No. 2) v. IFAD*, consideration 3, wherein the Tribunal held that the complainant was deprived of having her internal appeal properly examined because the Organization failed to provide her with the investigation report into her complaint of harassment. Also relevant is ILOAT Judgment 4739 (2024) *T. v. Global Fund to Fight AIDS, Tuberculosis and Malaria*, at considerations 10, 11, and 12, wherein the Tribunal confirmed its case law that the fact that the organization's rules do not provide for the disclosure of the investigation report does not absolve the Administration from the obligation to disclose the investigation report to a person reporting harassment. See also ILOAT Judgment 4862 (2024) *B. (No. 3) v. WHO/UNAIDS*, at consideration 6.

[35] See, for example, ILOAT Judgment No. 2475 (2005) *A.K.T.B. v. WHO*, consideration 7: "internal investigations should be conducted in a manner designed all relevant facts without compromising the good name of the employee [...]."

[36] See, for example, Judgment No. 4253 (2020) *Z. v. ILO*, consideration 3, wherein the Tribunal noted "the requirements of its case law with regard to investigations into harassment allegations: such investigations must be prompt and thorough, the facts must be established objectively and in their overall context, the law must be applied correctly, and due process must be observed (see Judgments 2642, consideration 8, and 3692, consideration 18)." See also Judgment No. 2973

begin promptly and be completed within a reasonable time.[37] In this regard, the Tribunal has repeatedly recognized that long delays compromise the integrity of the investigation process[38] and has awarded damages for undue delay.[39] The Tribunal has noted that it is for the organization to ensure the availability of appropriate and efficient investigative mechanisms.[40] According to one commentator, Donata Rugarabamu, the Tribunal is aware of the various administrative and bureaucratic challenges organizations face in implementing their internal rules and procedures, but such challenges do not furnish the organization with an incontestable excuse for delay.[41]

The ILOAT's jurisprudence also has it that the person alleging harassment bears the burden of proving their allegations.[42] While it is the investigator's role to collect

(2011) *B.K.M v. WHO*, consideration 14, noting that the Organization had put the interests of the alleged harasser over the claimant, the Tribunal held that: "the Organization has a duty to provide both sides with an equal opportunity to present their case and to challenge the positions being advanced by the other party to the dispute [. . .] the complainant has been denied the opportunity to challenge these statements or to adduce evidence in response." Citing earlier judgments, the Tribunal also noted that: "In Judgment 2552 the Tribunal pointed out that an accusation of harassment requires that an international organisation both investigate the matter thoroughly and accord full due process and protection to the person accused. Its duty to a person who makes a claim of harassment requires that the claim be investigated both promptly and thoroughly, that the facts be determined objectively and in their overall context [. . .], that the law be applied correctly, that due process be observed and that the person claiming, in good faith, to have been harassed not be stigmatised or victimised on that account [. . .]."

[37] See, for example, ILOAT Judgment No. 4241 (2020) *N. (No. 2) v. WHO*, consideration 4: "The Tribunal has consistently stated that harassment cases should be treated as quickly and efficiently as possible, in order to protect staff members from unnecessary suffering, but attention must also be paid to thoroughness and procedure (Judgment 3447, consideration) and that moral injury caused to the complainant by excessive delay will be fairly redressed by awarding her or him compensation (see, for example, Judgment 4111)."

[38] See, for example, ILOAT Judgment No. 2973 (2011) *B.K.M. v. WHO*, consideration 15, the Tribunal noted: "[. . .] the long delay seriously compromised the integrity of the investigation process. In addition to the diminishing recollection of events with the passage of time, potential witnesses are no longer available. As well, with the passage of time, it may be that those individuals in the Administration responsible for ensuring the protection of the staff member concerned are no longer with the Organization. If so, this would effectively preclude any accountability for the failure to protect a staff member if a finding of harassment were to be made."

[39] See ILOAT Judgment No. 4241 (2020) *N. (No. 2) v. WHO*, where the Tribunal awarded moral damages having found a delay of 9 months before the investigative body had called its first witness as too long, and excessively delaying the completion of the process.

[40] See ILOAT Judgment No. 4039 (2018) *K. v. ILO*, consideration 10 "[A]n international organisation has an obligation to initiate the investigation in a timely manner and the corollary obligation of ensuring that the internal body responsible for investigating and reporting on the allegations has the necessary resources to carry out that responsibility (see also Judgment 3347, under 14)." See also ILOAT Judgment No. 4471 (2022) *G. v. Eurocontrol*, considerations 9–11.

[41] Rugarabamu (2017) pp. 137–153.

[42] See, for example, ILOAT Judgment No. 4344 (2020) *A. (No. 2) v. IAEA*, consideration 3: "The Tribunal's case law states that the question as to whether harassment has occurred must be determined in the light of a thorough examination of all the objective circumstances surrounding

and assess the facts to the required standard of proof, under the ILOAT's case law to be given a fair chance to prove their allegations a claimant must have the opportunity to furnish evidence, including the ability to see and refute statements made and evidence introduced by the alleged perpetrator and witnesses during the investigation.[43] The Tribunal has presumably introduced this "adversarial" aspect into the investigation process because a claimant alleging harassment does not have a comparable right to subsequent proceedings in the same way as the alleged perpetrator, who typically under the disciplinary rules of international organizations is given the opportunity to challenge the investigation report before a decision is taken on any disciplinary measure.

As for the standard of proof required to give effect to the claimants' obligation to prove their allegations, the ILOAT clarified its position as it applies to harassment investigations in *G. M. v. IAEA (2020)*. The case involved a claim of sexual harassment found by the organization's investigative body to be unsubstantiated. The investigators had considered that the evidence (including after having interviewed some sixteen witnesses) was inadequate to conclude that the complainant's harassment was established "beyond a reasonable doubt." For the investigators the "beyond reasonable doubt standard" needed proof from independent witnesses present during the alleged incidents. The Tribunal found this reasoning flawed, holding that: *"[t]he Tribunal's case law states that the applicable standard of proof for a finding of harassment in a case such as this is not 'beyond reasonable doubt' but a less onerous standard."* In arriving at this ruling, the Tribunal stated that the legal relationship an organization has with the alleged perpetrator was "distinct and separate" from the legal relationship it had with the claimant, justifying a different standard of proof to conclude that the organization had failed in its duty of care towards the claimant to maintain a harassment-free workplace.[44] As Judge Bradley observes: *"[t]he ILOAT's ruling in G.M. v. IAEA implies that an international organization must necessarily have two distinct*

---

the events complained of and that an allegation of harassment must be borne out by specific facts, the burden of proof being on the person who pleads it. . ."

[43] In ILOAT Judgment No. 2654 (2007) *E.S.R. v. UNESCO*, consideration 7, the Tribunal made the following observation: "By failing to conduct an inquiry to determine the validity of such serious accusations, the defendant breached both its duty of care towards one of its staff members and its duty of good governance, thereby depriving the complainant of the right to be given an opportunity to prove her allegations. This attitude is liable to have caused serious injury which the indemnity awarded at the proposal of the Appeals Board does not entirely redress." See further ILOAT judgments cited in sect. 5 of this chapter.

[44] ILOAT Judgment No. 4207 (2020) at consideration 14: "A claim of harassment and a report of misconduct based on an allegation of harassment are distinct and separate matters. A claim of harassment is a claim addressed to the organization the resolution of which only involves two parties, the organization and the reporter of the harassment. In contrast a report of alleged misconduct, based on an allegation of harassment triggers [. . .] a process that is directed at the culpability of the staff member in question and potentially the imposition of a disciplinary measure. In this process, the two parties are the organization and the staff member in question. In this process the reporter of the misconduct, a potential victim of the harassment, is a witness and not a party in the proceedings."

procedures for dealing with harassment allegations, one for a claim for protection against such (alleged) behavior, another for dealing with the disciplinary investigation and punishment of harassment which has been found."[45]

According to Petrović: "*[w]hile the standard of proof required by the Tribunal for misconduct is 'beyond reasonable doubt', which is a relatively high bar, there has been a considerable misunderstanding that the same standard applies when determining whether harassment has occurred from the victim's perspective. The Tribunal has ruled that a lower standard must be met in the latter case.*"[46] The "less onerous" or "lower" standard the Tribunal referenced in the earlier judgment is that of the "balance of probabilities."[47] The Tribunal subsequently restated its position in another judgment holding that: "*[w]hile an allegation of harassment may found disciplinary proceedings in which the standard of 'beyond reasonable doubt' would apply, it has no application in the assessment of the claim of harassment where the staff member is seeking workplace protection or damages or both...*"[48]

These ILOAT judgments are welcome insofar as they recognize that the nature of harassment allegations makes it nearly impossible to establish the facts beyond a reasonable doubt. However, as Bradley observes: "*[t]he ILOAT's approach [...] could have the effect of undermining the value of the work of the body investigating the allegations.*"[49] This is because the organization normally relies on one investigative process to decide how it will respond to the claimant and the perpetrator. The ILOAT's approach will therefore undoubtedly add a new layer of complexity to the handling of harassment complaints as in deciding whether to take disciplinary action the organization must still be satisfied that the "beyond reasonable doubt standard"[50] is applied to the perpetrator.[51] By creating two standards for the same conduct, these judgments will make it more difficult for organizations to manage a harassment-free working environment. The potential consequence is that organizations may become

[45] Bradley (in press), this volume.

[46] Petrović (2021) pp. 190–191.

[47] See ILOAT Judgment No. 3725 (2017) *R. v. UNIDO*, consideration 14: "Essentially, IOS is a fact-finding investigative body. Its task is to collect, collate and analyse information objectively, impartially, fairly and with the highest degree of integrity and *to determine thereupon whether there is sufficient information to substantiate a complaint on a balance of probabilities*, examining both inculpatory and exculpatory information." (emphasis added).

[48] See ILOAT Judgment No. 4289 (2020) *S. v. ICGEB*, at consideration 10.

[49] Bradley (in press), this volume.

[50] In contrast, the UNAT jurisprudence has consistently applied a "clear and convincing" standard of evidentiary proof in all disciplinary cases. See, for example, UNAT Judgment No. 2013-UNAT-302, at para 29, citing Judgment No. 2011-UNAT-164 (Molari): "[W]hen termination is a possible outcome, misconduct must be established by clear and convincing evidence', which 'means that the truth of the facts asserted is highly probable'." See also Powers (2019).

[51] See ILOAT Judgment No. 3964 (2018) *F. S. v. EPO*: "[I]t is not for the Tribunal to assume the role of fact finder and determine, itself, whether the case is made out that the complainant was guilty of the misconduct alleged. Rather the Tribunal will review the evidence to determine whether 'a finding of guilt beyond a reasonable doubt could properly have been made by the primary trier of fact', in this case the President."

liable to victims of workplace harassment for injury caused to them, while the perpetrators remain unaccountable for their actions or possibly even awarded damages if the organization takes disciplinary measures, and the Tribunal sets aside the organization's decision as procedurally flawed.[52] This in turn may create the perception that the ILOAT and the organization required to implement the ILOAT's decision are protecting the perpetrator over the victim.

5 Due Process in Harassment Investigations

The potentially severe consequence to employees found to have committed misconduct has meant that, in the past, administrative tribunals and, consequently, the organizations were focused on the due process rights of the alleged perpetrator of misconduct otherwise known as the "subject" of the investigation. For example, it is widely recognized that an employee who is the subject of an investigation must be presumed innocent until such time a charge is properly established, and that the concerned individual must be given a genuine opportunity to challenge the accusations leveled against them before a disciplinary decision is taken. If the organization decides to initiate disciplinary proceedings in light of the findings of an investigation report, the alleged perpetrator must be given the opportunity to reply to the investigative findings so as to respect their right of defense. In harassment cases, this means that the alleged perpetrator must be informed of the basis of any charge of misconduct, and be given the name of their accuser(s) and the evidence gathered, where that evidence is the basis for the final determination on the allegations.[53] In the case of the alleged perpetrator who are typically protected under the organization's internal rules, due process rights apply "strictly" when (and if) disciplinary action is taken such that procedural safeguards omitted during the investigation could be rectified during any subsequent disciplinary proceedings.

---

[52] See ILOAT Judgment No. 4579 (2022) *M. v. Global Fund to Fight AIDS, Tuberculosis and Malaria*, in which the Tribunal ordered the reinstatement of the complainant who had been dismissed for sexual harassment as of the effective date of his dismissal.

[53] Powers (2015) pp. 166–169. See also, for example, ILOAT Judgment 4011 (2018) *N. v. FAO*, consideration 9, wherein the Tribunal reiterated the basic applicable principles regarding the right to due process at the investigative stage: "The general requirement with respect to due process in relation to an investigation – that being the function performed by the Investigation Panel in this case – is as set out in Judgment 2475, namely, that the 'investigation be conducted in a manner designed to ascertain all relevant facts without compromising the good name of the employee and that the employee be given an opportunity to test the evidence put against him or her and to answer the charge made'." Additionally, see UNAT Judgment No. 2021-UNAT-1146/Corr. 1, at para 57: "The essential question regarding procedural fairness is whether a staff member was adequately apprised of any allegations of misconduct and had a reasonable opportunity to make representations before action was taken against him. The [UNAT] is generally satisfied that the key elements of the rights of due process are met when the staff member was fully informed of the charges against him, the identity of his accusers and their testimony and as such, was able to mount a defense and to call into question the veracity of their statements."

On the other hand, the international jurisprudence, and the internal rules of international organizations, are generally less well developed when it comes to the due process rights of the claimants of workplace harassment. Joan S. Powers surveyed the case law of various international administrative tribunals and observed in 2018 that "general principles" cannot yet be said to have been established in relation to the rights of victims of workplace harassment.[54] Recent ILOAT judgments however indicate the emergence of case law on due process rights for claimants of workplace harassment applicable during the investigation process.

5.1 Claimants' Rights to "Test" the Evidence and Be Given an Opportunity to Prove Their Allegations

On the duty of care owed by an organization towards claimants of harassment, writing in 2015, Powers had noted "the beginnings of a trend" at the ILOAT, with Judgment No. 3065 (2012).[55] The case concerned a former official of the ILO who had accused her immediate supervisor of harassment. Her grievance was investigated, and her allegations found to be unsubstantiated. Before the Tribunal, the claimant argued that the adversarial principle was breached (citing an earlier Tribunal judgment involving a disciplinary matter[56]) insofar as the investigator had interviewed witnesses in her absence and without inviting her to attend the interviews or to comment on their written testimony. Relying on an earlier ruling,[57] the Tribunal considered that a complainant in a harassment investigation must be shown witness testimonies and be offered the opportunity to express disagreement and/or request that the information be rectified or to challenge the testimony by

[54] Powers (2019), pp. 117–118. Based on her review of various tribunals, Powers notes that "[w]ith respect to the rights of victims who lodge complaints of harassment or retaliation, this is a relatively new issue for the tribunals, such that it cannot be said that 'general principles' have been established."

[55] Powers (2015), p. 170.

[56] See ILOAT Judgment No. 1675 (1998) *In re Nivell, Eurocontrol*, consideration 6. The complainant in this case had been dismissed for "professional incompetence." A disciplinary board had been established and held an "adversarial inquiry." The board heard witnesses in the absence of the complainant. The Organization in question argued that the inquiry would be adversarial "if the [disciplinary board] hears witnesses called by both sides." The Tribunal rejected the argued holding that: "An inquiry will be adversarial only if the parties attend, or had been invited to attend, the hearing of witnesses" and ruled in favor of the complainant.

[57] See ILOAT Judgment No. 2973 (2011) *B. K.M. v. WHO/UNAIDS*, consideration 14. The complainant in this case had been denied a full investigation because the alleged offender was unwell and could not participate in the process. The Tribunal found that: "[by] terminating the investigation, WHO put the interests of the alleged harasser ahead of those of the complainant. . . the Organization has a duty to provide both sides with an equal opportunity to present their case and to challenge the positions being advanced by the other party to the dispute. . .the complainant has been denied the opportunity to challenge these statements or to adduce evidence in response."

furnishing further evidence.[58] The ILOAT ruled that the adversarial principle had been breached and awarded the complainant moral damages, finding that her due process rights had not been observed, and that the Organization had acted in breach of its duty of care towards her and its duty of good governance that resulted in the complainant being deprived of her right to be given an opportunity to prove her allegations.[59]

Since then, several ILOAT rulings have addressed the rights of claimants in harassment investigations. For example, in another judgment involving the ILO, the Tribunal found that the Organization had failed to provide the complainant (as well as the alleged perpetrator) in a harassment claim with all the evidence gathered during the preliminary fact-finding (including testimonies of witnesses interviewed). For the Tribunal "*[b]oth had the right to test and answer such evidence at that stage, including by giving evidence if they so wished. So far as concerns the complainant, the failure to provide her with that information constituted a serious breach of the requirements of due process.*"[60] In another case, the Tribunal found that the EPO had breached the adversarial principle in the context of a harassment investigation undertaken by the Organization's ombudsperson. Citing earlier judgments, the Tribunal found that the complainant had not been given an opportunity to refute negative statements that had been made against her by the person she had accused of harassment and a witness. The Tribunal considered that the complainant ought to have been allowed to see their testimony so that she might challenge it, if necessary, by furnishing evidence.[61]

Additionally, in a series of connected judgments delivered in 2019 involving ILO employees who brought a joint grievance against their manager, the ILOAT reiterated its position that a claimant in a harassment investigation must be given the opportunity to challenge all statements made by the alleged perpetrator and witnesses during the investigative process.[62] In these cases, the Tribunal set aside the organization's decisions because the claimants had not been provided with records of *all* interviews with the alleged offender and witnesses. This was irrespective of the discretion of the investigator as to the materiality of the information.

In other cases, the Tribunal's has taken a different approach to the applicability of the adversarial principle to claimants in harassment investigations. In *A. M. (No. 5) v. Eurocontrol* (2020),[63] the claimant argued that her right to be heard had not been respected during the investigation because she was not allowed to submit comments on the evidence gathered or to inspect the file compiled by the investigators before they completed their report. The Tribunal did not accept her arguments, holding that the investigators had not been required to provide the statements made by the

[58] ILOAT Judgment No. 3065 (2012) *R. M. v. ILO*, at considerations 7–8.

[59] Ibid., consideration 11.

[60] See ILOAT Judgment No. 3071 (2012) *O. F. v. ILO*, considerations 35–37.

[61] See ILOAT Judgment No. 3617 (2016) *G. v. EPO*, considerations 11–12.

[62] See ILOAT Judgments Nos. 4108, 4109, 4010, 4011 (2019), *ILO*, in all at consideration 4.

[63] ILOAT Judgment No. 4279.

accused or the witness testimonies. The Tribunal observed that the investigators had interviewed the complainant twice, once at the beginning of the process and a second time before the investigators completed their report, and that she had been provided with a sufficiently detailed summary of the report with the Organization's decision on her harassment complaint.[64] In *T. v. WHO* (2021),[65] a WHO official whose harassment complaint was not accepted by the organization argued inter alia that his right to be heard had been violated because he was not given the opportunity to comment on the draft investigation report. The Tribunal rejected the complainant's submission holding that: "*[i]n submitting the harassment complaint, the complainant was the reporter of a possible misconduct, a potential victim of the harassment and a witness. Given that the complainant, in this case, was not the subject of the investigation process and, therefore, was not in an adversarial situation [. . .], the principle of due process and the right to be heard are not applicable in these circumstances.*"[66]

Notwithstanding the inconsistency in the case law noted above, the ILOAT now appears to take the approach that employees alleging harassment have a due process right to know and challenge the evidence collected during the investigation into their harassment complaint. Certainly, the ILOAT seems to consider this due process right as part of its "settled case law." In *P. v. ILO* (2020),[67] the complainant contended that the organization's internal rules[68] and the adversarial principle were infringed because she was not given the opportunity to know the witnesses and respond to their testimony during the investigation process into her harassment grievance. The Tribunal accepted the argument holding that the witness testimonies were crucial items of evidence which formed the basis of the findings of the investigation report, and noted its "*settled case law according to which, in the context of an investigation into allegations of harassment, a complainant must have the opportunity to see the statements gathered in order to challenge or rectify them, if necessary, by furnishing evidence [. . .].*"[69] Other ILOAT judgments have since reflected the same approach.[70]

The ILOAT's case law on this topic presents a challenge to organizations and their investigative bodies who will need to decide how they are to give effect in practice to the adversarial principle in relation to employee(s) alleging workplace harassment. The ILOAT's approach is not clear on this aspect. Some of its

[64] Ibid., consideration 5.

[65] ILOAT Judgment No. 4378.

[66] Ibid., consideration 15.

[67] ILOAT Judgment No. 4313.

[68] The ILO's staff regulations provided that "both the claimant and the respondent are to be informed of witness testimony so that they can exercise their right of reply."

[69] Ibid., consideration 7.

[70] See ILOAT Judgment No. 4663 (2023) *M.-C. v. Interpol*, consideration 7 and ILOAT Judgment No. 4679 (2023) *C. v. ITER Organization*, consideration 5: "The case law requires that the person who lodged a harassment complaint be informed of the content of the interviews and be allowed to comment on them [. . .]."

rulings suggest that complainants in harassment investigations ought to be provided with written statements (presumably the records of interviews with the alleged offender and the witnesses) before concluding the investigation so that they be accorded the full opportunity to prove their allegations. The sharing of material evidence with the claimant before conclusions are drawn on the allegations is certainly essential to a thorough and fair investigative process. What is important however is that the information shared is that which the investigator relies on in support of their findings, and that the method and timing of sharing evidence remains within the discretion and judgment of the investigator. A general requirement to share all statements of the alleged perpetrator and witnesses, as appears to be the ILOAT's approach, may have far-reaching consequences not only on the timeliness of the process, but also on the wellbeing of the claimant (who may become privy to immaterial but harmful information about them) and on witnesses who may hesitate to speak the whole truth knowing that their testimony must be shared.

5.2 Claimants' Rights in Relation to Witnesses

Another relevant topic to the conduct of the investigation is the investigators' discretionary decision on who to call as witnesses. In one case before the Tribunal involving UNAIDS, the complainant argued that there was a lack of fairness, objectivity, and impartiality during the investigation process because the investigative body had not interviewed witnesses whom she suggested, including individuals at the highest level of the Organization's leadership. The complainant had identified twenty-four witnesses concerning various allegations of harassment. The investigative body interviewed seven of those and transmitted a summary of their testimony to the complainant. The investigators subsequently interviewed a further five witnesses. Relying on an earlier ruling,[71] the Tribunal found that the investigative body had not called "*some of the persons whom the complainant had identified concerning specific allegations, the UNAIDS Chief of Staff and the UNAIDS Executive Director in particular. This was in breach of proper procedure, particularly given that the [investigative body] had not explained why it did not hear those persons.*"[72]

Similarly, the complainant in *S. v. ILO* (2022)[73] argued that the investigator's decision to "*exclude some witnesses without any justification constitutes an arbitrary decision which vitiates the conclusions of the report.*"[74] The investigator had

[71] ILOAT Judgment No. 4111 (2019) *V. B. v. ILO*, at consideration 3, the Tribunal held that: "[a]ny administrative decision, even when the authority exercises discretionary power, must be based on valid grounds. In this case, the refusal without valid grounds, to hear witnesses with regard to the complainant's allegations constitutes breach of due process."

[72] See Judgment 4241 (2020) *N. (No. 2) v. WHO/UNAIDS*, consideration 11.

[73] ILOAT Judgment No. 4549.

[74] Ibid., consideration 6.

stated in the investigation report that "*[c]haracter witnesses and ex-employees were considered inappropriate individuals from whom evidence could be sought.*"[75] The Tribunal found the investigator's statement to be insufficient explanation and reasoned that had identified witnesses been interviewed, different conclusions might have been reached pointing to harassing conduct. Citing Judgment 4111, the Tribunal held that: "*[t]he failure, without valid grounds and notwithstanding the discretion conferred [by the Organization's Staff Regulations] to hear witnesses potentially supportive of the complainant's allegations constituted a breach of due process.*"[76] The failure to fully reason in the investigation report why witnesses proposed were not interviewed was sufficient to vitiate the validity of the report, such that the Organization's decision was set aside.

The ILOAT's case law seemingly therefore has it that investigators must now justify the reasons for not interviewing witnesses proposed by the claimants that they deem not to be material to the investigation. While it is essential for the investigative body to properly discharge its discretion in this regard to ensure a thorough and fair process, creating additional burdens and formalities on investigators risks unduly prolonging the process and, in combination with other requirements the ILOAT is increasingly imposing on the conduct of investigations, makes the process more involved and onerous for all stakeholders.

6 Conclusion

The focus in harassment cases before the ILOAT had previously been on the due process rights of the alleged perpetrator given the adverse effects that a finding of misconduct and disciplinary measures would have on them. With the rise in harassment complaints and the "speak up" culture in the wake of media reports of sexual misconduct, and given the duty of the organization to maintain a safe and respectful work environment, administrative tribunals are now increasingly concerned with the due process rights of the victims/claimants in harassment cases. Addressing both objectives is undoubtedly necessary. Investigations will inevitably involve investigators exercising judgment about a variety of competing factors, including the procedural safeguards that judicial bodies, such as the ILOAT, are identifying as necessary components of due process for both the complainant and the alleged perpetrator. In this context, pronouncements of the administrative tribunals, including the ILOAT, can support efforts to achieve robust investigations.

However, the increasing formalization of the internal investigation process, regardless of the type and severity of the allegations or the consequences for the individuals concerned, risks turning all fact-finding administrative processes into a fully-fledged adversarial and legalistic one, requiring additional resources and prolonging the negative impacts of the process on the parties and the wider working

[75] Ibid., consideration 8.

[76] Ibid., consideration 9.

environment. As a result, investigations into allegations of workplace harassment are becoming more and more resource and time-intensive undertakings affecting the well-being of employees—victims, alleged perpetrators, and witnesses alike—and often disrupting relationships within teams. This poses challenges to the shared aim of international organizations and their employees of effectively addressing allegations of improper behaviors through an investigative process that is objective, fair, and completed in a timely manner. The introduction of well-meaning due process standards for certain groups may pose challenges in managing the due process rights of others, as well as managing the ongoing work relationships between all employees who are involved in an investigation. In providing guidance to organizations in harassment cases, administrative tribunals should take into account the impact of introducing additional procedural requirements on the investigation process, the parties involved and all personnel affected by the case.

References

Bradley, K. (in press). Reasonable doubt about proof "beyond reasonable doubt" in international administrative law. In Bravo, T., Bradley, K. (eds), (this volume).

Petrović, D. (2021). How should harassment cases be dealt with in international organizations? A concise guide through the case law of the Administrative Tribunal of the International Labour Organization. In *New challenges of EAEU integration: The legal dimension*, Acts of international conference organised by the Court of Justice of the Eurasian Economic Union on 25–-27 November 2020, Minsk. Council of Europe (pp. 183–195).

Powers, J. S. (2015). Misconduct investigations and the disciplinary process: Balancing competing considerations of due process. In A. Talvik (Ed.), *Best practices in resolving employment disputes in International Organizations. Conference Proceedings 15–16 September 2014, ILO Geneva*. ILO Publication.

Powers, J. S. (2019). The evolving jurisprudence of the International Administrative Tribunals: Convergence or divergence? In P. Quayle & X. Gao (Eds.), *AIIB yearbook of international law* (p. 108). Koninklijke Brill NV.

Rugarabamu, D. (2017). Milestones in the jurisprudence of the International Labour Organization Administrative Tribunal: Guiding international organizations and their personnel in addressing harassment. In D. Petrović (Ed.), *90 Years of Contribution to the Administrative Tribunal of the International Labour Organization in the Creation of International Civil Service Law*. ILO Publication.

Waechter, M. (2012). Due process rights at the United Nations: Fairness and effectiveness in internal investigations. *International Organizations Law Review, 9*(2), 339–342.

The United Nations Jurisprudence on Pre-disciplinary Cases Involving Sexual Exploitation and Abuse

Eleanor Donaldson-Honeywell

Contents

1 Introduction 75
2 Procedural and Substantive Requirements for ALWP and ALWOP 78
3 Applications for Suspension of Action and Applications on the Merits 79
4 Legal Challenges at the SOA Stage 80
5 Substantive Issues in Pre-disciplinary Leave Decisions Affecting Staff Members Charged with SEA 82
6 Conclusion 83
Jurisprudence 84
Legal documents 85
Electronic resources 85

1 Introduction

The United Nations Dispute Tribunal ["UNDT"], established by the General Assembly in July 2009,[1] is one of the main entities in the three-tier formal system for determining challenges to administrative and disciplinary employment decisions

Eleanor J. Donaldson-Honeywell, Justice of Appeal at the Judiciary of Trinidad and Tobago and currently half time Judge with the UNDT. The views expressed are those of the author and not representative of the UNDT.

[1] Pursuant to GA Resolution A/RES/62/228.

E. Donaldson-Honeywell (✉)
UNDT, New York, NY, USA
e-mail: Eleanor.donaldson-honeywell@un.org

T. Bravo, K. Bradley (eds.), *Judicial Review in International Administrative Law*, Law for Professionals, https://doi.org/10.1007/978-3-031-71840-3_5

where informal resolution methods are exhausted: Management Evaluation Unit (MEU), UNDT, and United Nations Appeals Tribunal (UNAT).

These challenges arise from concerns as to non-compliance with staff members' terms of appointment, including all pertinent regulations and rules. The formal system, at the first instance adjudication level, is governed by the UN Staff Rules, as well as the Statute and Rules of Procedure of the UNDT.

As mentioned above, another of the main entities in the formal system is the management evaluation unit from which a staff member must first seek a management evaluation if the decision complained of is administrative.[2]

This step provides the Organization with an opportunity to review and correct an improper decision thereby, reducing the number of cases that proceed to formal litigation.

If the staff member remains aggrieved after management evaluation, the next recourse is formal litigation through an application to the UNDT[3] whose role in determining such applications is one of judicial review. In reviewing decision-makers' exercise of discretion in administrative matters, the Dispute Tribunal determines if the decision is legal, rational, procedurally correct, and proportionate. The Tribunal can consider whether relevant matters have been ignored and irrelevant matters considered and examine whether the decision is absurd or perverse.

The Tribunal is "more concerned with examining how the decision-maker reached the impugned decision and not the merits of the decision-maker's decision."[4]

Once the UNDT adjudicates the case, there may be recourse, by either party, to the third main entity in the formal system, by way of an appeal to the United Nations Appeals Tribunal ["UNAT"].[5]

Throughout its existence, the UNDT and UNAT have been called to adjudicate numerous complaints brought by staff members who are being investigated for sexual exploitation and abuse ["SEA"] and for alleged misconduct related to SEA.

In some of these cases, no final determination has yet been made by the Organization (Respondent), that there is clear and convincing evidence of any misconduct and, in some situations, the staff member may or may not have even had the opportunity to comment on the charges. Therefore, the affected staff member is awaiting the conclusion of investigations and a pending decision, which may or may not result in a disciplinary measure being imposed.

---

[2] UN Staff Rule 11.2.

[3] UN Staff Rule 11.4.

[4] *Sanwidi* 2010-UNAT-084, para 42, available at https://www.un.org/en/internaljustice/files/unat/judgments/2010-unat-084.pdf, accessed on 23 July 2024.

[5] Article 11.3 of the UNDT Statute.

The final determination on whether misconduct has occurred is an exercise of the Respondent's disciplinary functions, as detailed in the Staff Regulations and Rules[6] and it is part of a broader zero-tolerance policy[7] that the UN applies to SEA, which is defined as serious misconduct.[8]

The disciplinary measures which may be imposed at the end of an investigation vary, depending on the nature and seriousness of the misconduct at stake, but ultimately, it is recognized that, in cases of SEA a staff member may expect to be dismissed.[9]

On the other hand, in cases where the staff member has not been personally engaged in SEA but is being investigated for alleged misconduct on the periphery of SEA such as for non-reporting those facts, the sanction may range from very harsh to less severe. Failure to report has been seen to incur the harshest disciplinary measure of separation from service, almost as if the staff member accused of non-reporting was guilty of the sexual abuse or exploitation itself.

Other examples of the range of severe sanctions that the Administration can apply for non-reporting SEA are illustrated by *Loto* UNDT/2022/081 and *Owakol* UNDT/2022/082, where the applicants' employment was terminated. On the contrary, in *Kuya*,[10] another staff member alleged to be involved in the failure to report the same allegation of SEA was not dismissed. A differentiating factor in Kuya's involvement was that he played a subordinate role to the others when they all failed to report the matter while engaging the alleged victim and perpetrator in settlement talks.

There is however, one issue staff members face which usually gives rise to cases before the Tribunal at the pre-disciplinary sanction stage, i.e., regardless of the nature of the SEA allegation against them (whether their personal involvement is alleged or not), a Staff Member may be adversely affected by administrative measures, pending conclusion of a SEA investigation.

Those administrative measures, namely administrative leave with pay ["ALWP"] and even more so, administrative leave without pay ["ALWOP"] may have a severe personal and/ or professional impact on the staff member which may even be akin to, or worse than, the disciplinary measure that could be imposed at the end of the investigation.

Accordingly, careful consideration must be given to the procedural and substantive requirements that the Respondent must observe before the Tribunal upholds an ALWP or ALWOP decision.

---

[6] Staff Regulation 10 and Staff Rule 10.

[7] https://www.un.org/preventing-sexual-exploitation-and-abuse/content/response [accessed from United Nations website on 15 July 2024] and Secretary General's bulletin ST/SGB/2019/8.

[8] Staff Regulation 10.1(b).

[9] *Mbaigolmem* 2018-UNAT-819, para 33: "Sexual harassment is a scourge in the workplace which undermines the morale and well-being of staff members subjected to it. [. . .] The message therefore needs to be sent out clearly that staff members who sexually harass their colleagues should expect to lose their employment." Available at https://www.un.org/en/internaljustice/files/unat/judgments/2018-UNAT-819.pdf, accessed on 23 July 2024.

[10] See at https://www.un.org/internaljustice/oaj/en/judgment/undt2021134, accessed on 23 July 2024.

2 Procedural and Substantive Requirements for ALWP and ALWOP

ALWP and ALWOP are two different types of administrative decisions that the Respondent is authorized to apply to staff members, according to the UN's legal framework, before the conclusion of disciplinary investigations and proceedings. Among those, administrative leave with partial pay [ALWPP] may also be considered.

The regulatory underpinning of the Respondent's said authority contemplates different ranges of severity. Nonetheless, those administrative decisions, though severe, are conceptually different from disciplinary decisions.

Unlike disciplinary decisions, ALWP, ALWOP, and ALWPP were not intended to be imposed punitively although in practice this punitive dimension cannot be overlooked. As explained by UNAT in *Richard Loto 2022-UNAT-1292* at para 64, the Respondent's discretion in deciding to place staff members on leave, pending determination of disciplinary charges, is not unfettered.

> Under the applicable legal framework, in cases of misconduct the Secretary-General is not at complete liberty to place a staff member on ALWOP, as his discretion to do so is conditioned upon the existence of exceptional circumstances which, in instances of misconduct other than those concerning SEA, requires that: (1) the unsatisfactory conduct is of such gravity that it would, if established, warrant separation or dismissal under Staff Rule 10.2 (a) (viii) or (ix); and (2) there is information before the authorized official about the unsatisfactory conduct that makes it more likely than not (preponderance of the evidence) that the staff member engaged in the unsatisfactory conduct.

The applicable regulatory framework states as follows:

> Staff Rules
>
> **Rule 10.4**
>
> **Administrative leave pending investigation and the disciplinary process**
>
> (a) A staff member may be placed on administrative leave, subject to conditions specified by the Secretary-General, at any time after an allegation of misconduct and pending the completion of a disciplinary process. Administrative leave may continue until the completion of the disciplinary process.
>
> (b) A staff member placed on administrative leave pursuant to paragraph (a) above shall be given a written statement of the reason(s) for such leave and its probable duration.
>
> (c) Administrative leave shall be with full pay except (i) in cases in which there is probable cause that a staff member has engaged in sexual exploitation and sexual abuse, or (ii) when the Secretary-General decides that exceptional circumstances exist which warrant the placement of a staff member on administrative leave with partial pay or without pay.
>
> (d) Placement on administrative leave shall be without prejudice to the rights of the staff member and shall not constitute a disciplinary measure. If administrative leave is without pay and either the allegations of misconduct are subsequently not sustained or it is subsequently found that the conduct at issue does not warrant dismissal or separation, any pay withheld shall be restored without delay.
>
> (e) A staff member who has been placed on administrative leave may challenge the decision to place him or her on such leave in accordance with chapter XI of the Staff Rules.

The above-mentioned framework needs to be interpreted in conjunction with ST/AI/2017/1—Section 11, which reads, in its relevant parts, as follows:

> Administrative leave
>
> 11.1 In accordance with staff rule 10.4, a staff member may be placed on administrative leave with or without pay at any time after an allegation of suspected unsatisfactory conduct and pending the completion of the disciplinary process. The period of administrative leave may continue until the completion of the disciplinary process. Such action is without prejudice to the rights of the staff member and does not constitute a disciplinary measure. A staff member placed on administrative leave shall be given a written statement of the reason(s) for such leave and shall be informed of its likely duration.
>
> Administrative leave without pay
>
> 11.4 A staff member may be placed on administrative leave without pay by an authorized official when at least one of the following conditions is met:
>
> (a) There are reasonable grounds to believe (probable cause) that the staff member engaged in sexual exploitation and sexual abuse, in which case the placement of the staff member on administrative leave shall be without pay;
>
> (b) There are exceptional circumstances that warrant the placement of the staff member on administrative leave without pay because the unsatisfactory conduct is of such gravity that it would, if established, warrant separation or dismissal under staff rule 10.2 (a) (viii) or (ix), and there is information before the authorized official about the unsatisfactory conduct that makes it more likely than not (preponderance of the evidence) that the staff member engaged in the unsatisfactory conduct.

3 Applications for Suspension of Action and Applications on the Merits

Procedural issues concerning ALWP and ALWOP are usually first raised with the Tribunal in applications for the suspension of actions ["SOA"], i.e., before there has been a response by the organization to the staff member's management evaluation request.

An SOA application is akin to an application for injunctive relief in which the affected staff member is seeking immediate lifting of the administrative action.

The UNDT's jurisdiction to grant SOA orders is provided at Staff Rule 11.3, Article 10.1 of the UNDT Statute, and Articles 13–14 of the UNDT Rules of Procedure. An SOA order can be granted either pending management evaluation or pending substantive determination of an application by the UNDT, through *interim measures*.

SOA orders are usually not subject to appeal.[11] Accordingly, once a staff member's request challenging ALWP or ALWOP has been granted, he/she no longer suffers the consequences of said administrative decisions pending the outcome of management evaluation.

[11] UNDT Rules of Procedure, Articles 13.4 and 14.4.

The second situation referred to above—*interim measures relief* takes place when the Tribunal is seized of a substantive application challenging ALWP or ALWOP for determination on the merits, in the context of a disciplinary case.

Selected decisions of the UN Tribunals on SOA applications (which are not appealable) and on substantive applications shed light on the approach taken and are examined below.

4 Legal Challenges at the SOA Stage

In *Minaeva,* Order No. 56 (GVA/2020), Bravo J explained the cumulative requirements for SOA to be granted, as follows:

> 15. Applications for suspension of action are governed by art. 2.2 of the Tribunal's Statute and art. 13 of its Rules of Procedure, which provide that the Tribunal may suspend, during the pendency of the management evaluation, the implementation of a contested administrative decision that is the subject of an ongoing management evaluation, where the decision appears prima facie to be unlawful, in cases of particular urgency and where its implementation would cause irreparable damage.
>
> 16. For an application for suspension of action to be successful, it must satisfy the following mandatory and cumulative conditions:
>
> a. The Applicant requested management evaluation of the contested decision, which evaluation is ongoing;
> b. **The contested decision has not yet been implemented;**
> c. The application concerns an administrative decision that may be properly suspended by the Tribunal;
> d. The impugned administrative **decision appears prima facie to be unlawful;**
> e. Its implementation would cause irreparable damage; and
> f. The case is of particular urgency. [Emphasis added]

In addition to the requirements highlighted above, issues of receivability are often raised by the Respondent in applications seeking to suspend ALWP or ALWOP.

The Tribunal must then consider whether the application is receivable under Staff Rule 11.2(a) which provides that:

> A staff member wishing to formally contest an administrative decision alleging non-compliance with his or her contract of employment or terms of appointment, including all pertinent regulations and rules pursuant to staff regulation 11.1 (a), shall, as a first step, submit to the Secretary-General in writing a request for a management evaluation of the administrative decision.

This requirement is not always met as there are cases where an applicant may have been subject to repeated extensions of ALWP or ALWOP and overlooked the need to file separate management evaluation requests for each extension.

In those circumstances, UNAT jurisprudence in the case of *Gisage* 2019-UNAT-973 is relevant as the Appeals Tribunal explained the reason for finding an extension of the ALWOP to be a separate administrative decision. In para 30, the Appeals Tribunal explained that:

The facts taken into consideration at that stage were different. As such, the decision to extend the ALWOP was based on a fresh assessment and constituted a separate decision.

Consequently, the Tribunal must determine whether, in the circumstances of the case before it, the applicant's failure to file more than one management evaluation request (one per each extension) renders the application for suspension of the administrative leave unreceivable.

In the cases below, the UNDT addressed, through non-appealable Orders, the subject matter of receivability, as follows:

Antoine Order No. 172 (NBI/2020)[12]

The applicant was placed on ALWOP until the completion of investigations and any disciplinary process when a "video appeared on social media showing two male individuals and a female individual driving along a busy street in a clearly marked United Nations vehicle. The video captured one of the male individuals and the female in the back seat engaged in what appeared to be an act of a sexual nature as the vehicle was driven along a heavily trafficked street."

In her ruling granting suspension of action "to the extent it seeks to suspend the 'unpaid' aspect of administrative leave" Judge Millart stated several considerations which, since then, are quoted in similar SOA cases, as follows:

Para 26 – "Staff rule 10.4(c) confirms that ALWOP, which departs from the fundamentals of the employment relation, is an exceptional measure and not a matter of vast administrative discretion. Consequently, application of ALWOP requires, primarily, the Respondent to show that legal premises allowing it are fulfilled."

Para 27 – "For staff rule 10.4(c)(i) to be applicable it would be necessary that a staff member's actions were, at a minimum, accessory to sexual abuse or sexual exploitation."

Para 29 – "Under staff rule 10.4(c)(ii), the Respondent is required to show why administrative leave is necessary, moreover, what legitimate interest necessitates that it be without pay."

Loto Order No. 119 (NBI/2020)[13]

In this case, the applicant was placed on ALWOP pending the conclusion of investigations concerning SEA-related allegations. These included the fact that he failed to report an allegation of rape (made to him) concerning two other co-workers.

The duration of his ALWOP was initially three months, then there was a break and it was extended retroactively.

---

[12] See at https://www.un.org/en/internaljustice/files/undt/orders/nbi-2020-172.pdf, accessed on 23 July 2024.

[13] See at https://www.un.org/en/internaljustice/files/undt/orders/nbi-2020-119.pdf, accessed on 23 July 2024.

Tibulya J addressed issues of receivability as the Respondent contended that the first three-month period was fully implemented and therefore, said decision could no longer be suspended by the Tribunal.

In her ruling (paras 15–17) the Respondent's argument was not upheld because, as stated therein "the Respondent's clear intention was to seamlessly connect the two decisions, and indeed as argued by the Applicant, the 13 May 2020 extension of the ALWOP was not a standalone decision and it does not exist on its own without the original 13 January 2020 decision."

Accordingly, the Respondent was ordered to change the ALWOP decision to ALWP, retroactively, to coincide with the beginning of the first ALWOP period.

As a consequence, the Applicant's full pay and entitlements should be reinstated for that period, as further reiterated by another Judge of the same tribunal in a similar case.[14]

Okwakol Order No. 127 (NBI/2020)[15]

In this case, as in *Loto*, Judge Milart also considered the question of receivability in deciding on an SOA application by an applicant being investigated for alleged misconduct arising from the same incident.

In *Okwakol,* the Tribunal stated that:

> 11. The subject of the application is a decision dated 13 May 2020 on the extension of ALWOP. It is clearly a discrete administrative decision, in a nexus with the decision that applied the ALWOP in the first place, but reviewable in and of itself. Only this decision may be subject to the Tribunal's order, whatever it might be.

5 Substantive Issues in Pre-disciplinary Leave Decisions Affecting Staff Members Charged with SEA

When the Tribunal is adjudicating on the substantive merits of a case, the Applicant's success depends on the scope and limits of judicial review.

These were summarized by Judge Tibulya in *Antoine* UNDT/2021/151 at para 29 as follows:

> ...in conducting judicial review of decisions to place an applicant on ALWOP, the Dispute Tribunal reviews whether the decision was lawful and rational, considering the criteria stipulated in the Staff Rules and ST/AI/2017/1 and the information before the head of entity at the time of the decision. It is not for the Dispute Tribunal to substitute its own view for the head of entity's decision, but to evaluate whether that decision was irrational or arbitrary

[14] See Order No. 132 (NBI/2020) at https://www.un.org/en/internaljustice/files/undt/orders/nbi-2020-132.pdf, accessed on 23 July 2024.

[15] See *Okwakol* 2022-UNAT-1293 at https://www.un.org/internaljustice/oaj/en/judgment/2022-unat-1293, accessed on 23 July 2024.

In recently adjudicated cases by UNAT, relevant considerations were expressed concerning Applicants challenging ALWOP, pending SEA investigations.

As mentioned, in *Okwakol*, UNAT observed that:

> 51. While ALWOP is not a disciplinary sanction, its effects on a staff member, especially in cases involving a prolonged investigation, can be detrimental and in some ways at least as, or even more, detrimental than severance from service. That is because, while the staff member on ALWOP remains an employee of the Organization, he or she cannot earn an income, whether from the United Nations or elsewhere. An attempt to earn remuneration for work for another employer is generally prohibited by the Organization. Moreover, the staff member is restricted as to where he or she can travel while on ALWOP; thus, even though not required there for the performance of work, he or she cannot leave the relevant duty station without the consent of the Organization. That is more than an insignificant constraint on the right of freedom of movement. The staff member may also be without accommodation if such housing is part of their role.
>
> 52. While it is also true that, if subsequently vindicated, a staff member placed on ALWOP will recover some or all of his/her lost remuneration, that often cannot save the consequences of previous impecuniosity attributable to the absence of income.
>
> 53. The consequences of being on ALWOP are not only economic. The shame, stigma, humiliation, loss of dignity and other similar less tangible but nevertheless real consequences attaching to being suspected of serious misconduct are residual and oppressive. That may be so even if the staff member is eventually found to have been innocent of these serious charges. 54. While the emphasis placed by the Organization on the identification and elimination of SEA is very important, so too are the human and due process rights of staff members who have not yet at least, been adjudged guilty of that misconduct. These factors must be carefully balanced in making decisions about administrative leave and particularly if this is to be without pay and for prolonged periods.

Ultimately, UNAT ruled against the Applicant in *Okwakol* as he admitted he had erred by failing to end a meeting when he discovered that it involved negotiations with a complainant alleging she was raped.

UNAT held, "*Not only was Mr. Okwakol remiss in not ending the meeting when these matters emerged, but he was bound to, but did not, report his concerns or suspicions which he should have held following those revelations. ...The Administration was entitled to assume that this was unsatisfactory conduct and of such gravity that, if established in the investigation, would warrant separation or dismissal.*"

From the Appeals Tribunal's point of view, the Administration was entitled to find it was "more likely than not" that *Okwakol* committed misconduct (for not reporting SEA) and this was considered to be "prima facie" sufficient to justify his administrative leave without pay.

6 Conclusion

Imposing measures such as ALWP and ALWOP can be quite draconian due to their severe impact on staff members. Accordingly, Tribunals must ensure that such measures are imposed only in the appropriate circumstances in a manner that is procedurally correct and in accordance with the regulatory framework and due process standards.

Moreover, as recognized by UNAT in *Gisage 2019-UNAT-973* at para 40, any decision to extend ALWOP is a drastic administrative measure that normally should be of short duration.

It is worth noting though, that further developments in this area arise from clarifications provided by recent UNAT decisions in *Loto* and *Okwakol.*

However, any reduction in the severity of the potential impact of ALWOP on staff members is a matter of legislative action and change in policy that can only be meaningfully addressed through amendments to the legal framework. The time may well be right for a consideration of such amendments.

In the current legal framework, the presumption is that administrative leave will be on full pay (ALWP). That default position is subject to exceptions[16] where ALWOP or with partial pay may be implemented.

A valuable step towards reform could clarify that, as a prelude to ALWOP, the organization should first consider whether partial pay would be more appropriate, taking into consideration factors such as the staff member's personal status, his/her living expenses, and family responsibilities.

Another element that ought, in my view, to be considered, should amendments to the legal framework be deemed desirable, is the need to afford staff members due process rights. This must be balanced with the interests of the organization in furthering the zero-tolerance approach to SEA, by ensuring that, only in exceptional and severe cases the organization and its member states are relieved from salary payment obligations.

Jurisprudence

Appeals Tribunal

- 2010/UNAT/084
- 2018/UNAT/819
- 2019/UNAT/973
- 2022/UNAT/1293

United Nations Dispute Tribunal

- UNDT/NBI/2020/49
- UNDT/NBI/2022/081

Orders

- Order No. 172/NBI/2020
- Order No. 119/NBI/2020
- Order No. 132/NBI/2020
- Order No. 127/NBI/2020

[16] See *Okwakol*, footnote 15.

Legal documents

- General Assembly Resolution A/RES/62/228
- Statute of the United Nations Dispute Tribunal, 24 December 2008 (as amended 22 December 2018)
- Rules of Procedure of the United Nations Dispute Tribunal, 16 December 2009
- UN Staff Regulations and Rules ST/SGB/2018/1/Rev.2
- UN Administrative Instruction on Unsatisfactory Conduct, Investigations and the Disciplinary Process, ST/AI/2017/1
- Secretary General's Bulletin ST/SGB/2019/18

Electronic resources

- https://www.un.org/internaljustice/oaj/en

Divergent Standards of Proof Currently Applied by International Administrative Tribunals in Serious Misconduct Cases: An Evolving Snapshot

T. Michael Peay

Contents

1 Introduction 87
2 A Comparative Snapshot of Divergent Standards of Proof in Current IAT Practice 88
2.1 Adherents to the Preponderance of Evidence/Balance of Probabilities/51% Tests 88
3 IAT Adherents to the "Substantial Evidence" Test 94
4 IAT Adherent to the "Established and Substantiated" Test 95
5 IAT Adherents to the "Clear and Convincing Evidence" Test 96
6 The Administrative Tribunal of the Organization of American States (OASAT) 99
7 IAT Adherents to the "Beyond a Reasonable Doubt" Standard 102
8 To Strike a Fair Balance Between the Staff's vs. the Institution's Interests 103
9 What Provisional Conclusions Can be Drawn from this Snapshot Survey? 104
9.1 "Serious" vs. "Lesser" (or "More Routine") Misconduct 105
10 Closing Observations 106

1 Introduction

In May 2022, the IDBAT (the Inter-American Development Bank Administrative Tribunal) in Washington, D.C. hosted a colloquium to mark its 40th anniversary. On that occasion, the author, in his then capacity as Vice President of the Organization of American States (OAS) Administrative Tribunal, presented a short paper and remarks focusing on a comparative review of practice at several select IATs with

T. Michael Peay, former Judge and President of the Administrative Tribunal of the Organization of American States.

T. M. Peay (✉)
Administrative Tribunal of the Organization of American States, Washington, DC, USA

T. Bravo, K. Bradley (eds.), *Judicial Review in International Administrative Law*, Law for Professionals, https://doi.org/10.1007/978-3-031-71840-3_6

regard to the standards of proof they currently apply in reviewing disciplinary cases that involve findings of serious misconduct. This article builds upon and extends that research and those remarks, but does not purport to be an exhaustive review of all current tribunal case law on this subject. Rather, as noted in the Abstract, it seeks to offer an illustrative snapshot of selective contemporary practice.

An underlying assumption of this article is that most legal, even non-legal, observers would agree that "*misconduct*" cases tend to provoke a unique visceral reaction, most likely due to the stigma inherently associated with the term "*misconduct.*" Possible irreparable reputational injury, career damage, as well as physical and mental harm are among the collateral consequences that can result from an accusation and finding of workplace "*misconduct.*"

For these reasons, such cases can readily be seen as qualitatively different from other types of workplace disputes, like those concerning: pension rights; expiration of fixed-term contracts; reclassification of a post; or termination due to redundancy, among other examples that could be cited. Fortunately, these latter cases tend to arise more frequently before administrative tribunals. This is not at all to say or to suggest that those disputes are *ipso facto* less important than "*serious misconduct*" cases; only that, qualitatively speaking, they are less likely to arouse similar human reactions.

Assuming the foregoing assumptions have validity, it is reasonable to understand that "*misconduct cases*" deserve to receive *heightened judicial scrutiny* to ensure that the underlying facts in each case fully and objectively support both the "misconduct" alleged *and* the corresponding sanction imposed. *A fortiori* must this be true where the proposed disciplinary sanction is severe—summary dismissal or termination of employment.

With those preliminary thoughts in mind, the following is a comparative analysis offering examples of divergent standards of proof currently being applied in serious misconduct cases by a select group of 11 international administrative tribunals. These IATs are grouped according to the standard that they share in common. For added interest, they were chosen from diverse regions of the world.

2 A Comparative Snapshot of Divergent Standards of Proof in Current IAT Practice

2.1 Adherents to the Preponderance of Evidence/Balance of Probabilities/51% Tests[1]

The **Asian Development Bank Administrative Tribunal** (**AsDBAT**) applied the "*preponderance of evidence*" test in two 2013 serious misconduct companion decisions.[2] *Hua Du No. 1* involved the dismissal from employment of a senior

[1] In the UK, the "*preponderance*" test is often referred to as the "*balance of probabilities*" or "*51%*" test.

[2] *Hua Du No. 1* (AsDBAT Decision 101) and *Hua Du No.2* (AsDBAT Decision 102).

Bank official accused of helping to draft and circulate externally embarrassing emails that were critical of both the Bank as an institution and of certain senior Bank officials. Applying the "*preponderance*" test, the Tribunal upheld the Bank's finding that the accused was culpable of the serious misconduct alleged.

The two *Hua Du* cases are characterized as "interesting" for several reasons. First, in *Hua Du No. 1* the Tribunal *did not* judicially select and apply the "*preponderance*" test as the relevant *court-mandated* standard of proof. Rather, that standard's application was pre-ordained, made compulsory by an internal Administrative Order (AO 2.04) that governs the Bank's disciplinary proceedings.[3] Paragraph 8.1 of that AO provides that for such proceedings, "*(t)he standard of proof [...] is a Preponderance of Evidence.*" The Tribunal dutifully applied that standard and, in the process, also alluded to Appendix 1 of the Administrative Order, which defines "preponderance of evidence" as, "*Evidence which is more credible and convincing than that presented by the other party. In cases of misconduct, it is a standard of proof requiring that the Evidence as a whole show that it is more probable than not that the staff member committed the misconduct.*"[4]

The *Hua Du No. 1* Tribunal concluded in its opinion that the evidence before it showed that it was "*more probable than not that the applicant had knowledge of and was involved in [circulating the emails] and committed the misconduct with which she was charged.*"[5]

Second, the two *Hua Du* decisions are additionally interesting because of what happened when the initial decision was appealed to that Tribunal, this time sitting en banc (*Hua Du No. 2,* Decision 102, 2013). As noted earlier, the initial Tribunal panel that decided *Hua Du No. 1* was clearly *bound* by the Bank's internal law to apply the *preponderance of evidence* test.

That fact notwithstanding, the Appellant sought to convince the en banc Tribunal that the initial panel had applied an erroneous standard, arguing that reliance upon the "preponderance" test "*was contrary to the well-established standard of proof in misconduct cases which held that 'the standard of evidence in disciplinary decisions leading* [...] *to sanctions must be higher than a mere balance of probabilities'*" [citing *Dambita*, World Bank AT, Decision No. 243 (2001), para 21.][6] The appellant further contended that, "*[T]here should be clear proof beyond suspicion before a finding of guilt.*"[7] Not surprisingly, the en banc *Hua Du* (No. 2) Tribunal

[3]It is worth noting that the AsDB's Administrative Order 2.04 is the only instance the author uncovered in his research in which an internal institutional regulation expressly controls the applicable standard that its Tribunal is bound to apply in serious misconduct cases. A curious practical effect of this anomaly is that—until such a regulation is amended or rescinded by policymakers—it will continue to constrain what is normally a tribunal's unbridled judicial discretion to independently determine the appropriate legal standard to apply in such cases.

[4]*Hua Du No. 1* at para 39.

[5]Ibid., at para 40. See, also, AsDB AT Decision 107, *Ms. G. v. AsDB* [No. 2], at para 66 (2016).

[6]*Hua Du* (No. 2) at para 3.

[7]*Hua Du* (No. 2) at para 5.

unanimously rejected these assertions and denied the Applicant's request to reverse the first panel's decision or apply a new standard.

The fact that, on appeal, counsel brazenly attempted to assert that "*clear proof beyond suspicion*" was the appropriate standard of proof, and not that mandated by Administrative Order 2.04, seems to reflect growing awareness by attorneys that IAT practice in this regard is incrementally evolving towards adopting higher standards of proof than merely "preponderance" for serious misconduct cases.

The **Council of Europe Administrative Tribunal** (**ATCE**) also applies the "*preponderance of evidence*" standard, which it affirmed in a recent serious misconduct case, *B. v. COE.*[8] There, the staff member was accused of systematic abusive conduct. Applying the preponderance test, the Tribunal upheld a finding by the Director of Internal Oversight (DIO) that "*there was sufficient evidence to conclude that **it was more probable than not** that the appellant's behavior [had] breached the Organization's internal rules and that [his] behavior amounted to harassment and ... prohibited conduct*" sufficient *to* warrant his demotion in managerial status from level A4 to level A3.[9]

The Tribunal explained that the facts on which the disciplinary sanction was based "*[had] been established in part by the DIO's inquiry, and then refined and substantiated by the [Council of Europe's] Commission against Harassment.*" It therefore concluded that the record before it "[*provided] objective evidence of the matters for which the appellant was charged and sanctioned and ... sufficed to reach the standard of proof required in these matters.*" *[Emphasis added]*[10]

The **African Development Bank Administrative Tribunal** (**AfDBAT**) (like its Asian Development Bank and Council of Europe counterparts) has also adopted the "*preponderance*" or "*probabilities*" standard in reviewing serious misconduct cases. This has been observed in two notable AfDBAT decisions. In the first,[11] the sanction imposed was termination of employment, and, in the second, one of the sanctions was immediate demotion to lower managerial status.[12]

The misconduct alleged in the first case, Decision 96 (*E.O. v. African Development Bank*), concerned the leaking of a highly sensitive internal legal memo that contained privileged information relating to a then-ongoing internal Bank investigation into possible fraud and corruption involving an outside firm that was doing business with the Bank. A preliminary investigation into the leak produced prima facie evidence that implicated both the Applicant and an office colleague (whose case was separately handled). Based on that evidence, the Bank decided to open a fuller investigation and to provisionally suspend the Applicant.

---

[8] ATCE, Appeal 651 (2020).

[9] Ibid., *B. v. COE*, at para 10 [emphasis added].

[10] Ibid., at para 165.

[11] AfDBAT Decision 96, *EO v. AfDB* (2016).

[12] AfDBAT Decision 150, *J.O.L. v. AfDB* (2020). While demotion in managerial status is clearly less draconian than summary dismissal or termination, it is still severe enough to have a major adverse career impact.

That investigation lasted 16 months but failed to produce any *direct* evidence linking the Applicant to the leak. The Bank readily acknowledged that it bore the burden of proof and that, "*the standard of proof required in a case such as this is proof on a balance of probabilities*."[13] However, the Bank complained that the Applicant's refusal to cooperate with the investigation, by asserting a right to privacy, unfairly impeded the Bank's ability to prove that standard, and inferred her complicity in the leak and other related misconduct. The Bank therefore found sufficient *circumstantial evidence* of her culpability to justify her dismissal. That decision was then appealed to the AfDBAT.

The Tribunal's *ratio decidendi* in upholding the dismissal is notable. In the "*Burden and Standard of Proof*" section of its decision, the Tribunal explained:

> Insofar as the burden of proof is concerned, the burden will generally be on an Applicant to establish the merits of his or her application. However, where the application involves the termination of the employment of a Bank employee, the burden will be on the Bank to establish a *prima facie* case that the employee committed misconduct justifying dismissal, following which the burden shifts to the employee to rebut the evidence against him or her: *N.O. v. African Development Bank*, Application No. 2007/04.[14]
>
> With respect to the standard of proof, the parties agree this is not a criminal proceeding and that the Bank does not have to establish the Applicant's guilt beyond all reasonable doubt. *It is sufficient if the Bank can establish on a balance of probabilities that it had just cause to terminate the Applicant's employment.* While mere suspicion or speculation will not be enough, direct evidence of misconduct is not required. ***Cogent circumstantial evidence*** *that reasonably leads to a conclusion of guilt may be sufficient to establish misconduct justifying the termination of the employment of a Bank employee.*[15] [Emphasis added]

Applying those criteria to the facts of this case, the Tribunal surprisingly held that:

> While the actions of the Applicant in this case were undoubtedly suspicious when taken together, mere suspicions are not enough to establish guilt in a case such as this. Consequently, *the Tribunal is prepared to give the Applicant the benefit of the doubt, and to find that insufficient evidence has been adduced by the Bank* to establish her complicity in the leak of the [Bank's confidential legal memorandum] *on a balance of probabilities.*[16] [Emphasis added]

Yet, despite this finding and despite the absence of *sufficient* ***direct*** *evidence* to affirm the Applicant's misconduct—while at the same time applying a strict balance of probabilities test—the Tribunal ultimately fashioned a final decision that took into account the totality of the facts and circumstances. For the Applicant's protracted 16-month suspension, the Tribunal awarded damages of $5000.00 for the Bank's "egregious" breach of the Staff Rules.[17]

---

[13] Ibid., Decision 96 at para 65 [emphasis added].

[14] Ibid., Decision 96 at para 78.

[15] Ibid., at para 79.

[16] Ibid., at para 116.

[17] Ibid., para 95.

And interestingly, despite the admitted insufficiency of direct evidence of guilt, the Tribunal nevertheless *upheld the Bank's decision to dismiss the Applicant*, explaining its reasoning as follows:

> How could the Bank have continued confidence in the Applicant's work as a Principal Integrity and Prevention Officer when she herself had endeavored to obstruct a Bank investigation into an egregious breach of solicitor and client privilege that had the potential to cause enormous damage to the Bank in relation to the [on-going] investigation? The answer is clear: it could not. The actions of the Applicant in obstructing the investigation into the leak of the [confidential legal] opinion represented a fundamental breach of the duty of loyalty that the Applicant owed to the Bank, and justified the termination of her employment for misconduct.
>
> The Bank has thus established a *prima face* case that the Applicant committed misconduct justifying her dismissal for cause, and the Applicant has failed to rebut the evidence against her.[18]

Some may regard this outcome as schizophrenic, while others as may see it as Solomonic, conscientious, and just. As a practical matter, the Tribunal managed, both indirectly and creatively, to apply a unique version of the "*probabilities*" standard to the facts of this case, despite the absence of a body of direct evidence of culpability. It did so by fusing two otherwise separate standards of proof:

(i) the *prima facie* standard (which the Tribunal deemed had produced sufficient facts to establish the Applicant's culpable misconduct); and,
(ii) the "*cogent circumstantial evidence,*"[19] test (which it deemed to be sufficient to justify the Applicant's dismissal as a proportionate and thus lawful sanction).

It is interesting, however, to compare the AfDB Tribunal's ruling in Decision 96 with its ruling in another recent serious misconduct case (Decision 150),[20] where it explicitly applied the "*balance of probabilities*" test. There, an employee was charged with misconduct for allegedly: (i) having engaged in insubordination and (ii) filing a malicious workplace harassment (including sexual harassment) complaint against her supervisor.

Here, summary dismissal was not the impugned administrative sanction but rather several others: (i) *a written warning of dismissal,* if such act(s) were to recur; (ii) reassignment to another department; (iii) a demotion; and (iv) a 15% reduction of her current annual base salary.

Upon review, however, the AfDB Tribunal found that the principal charge (insubordination) had *not* been proven, using the "*balance of probabilities*" test. Moreover, the harassment complaint had not been filed maliciously but rather in good faith. In explaining its decision, the Tribunal opined that, "*The standard of proof is not proof beyond reasonable doubt as in criminal cases but is on a balance*

[18] See African DB Administrative Tribunal Decision 96, *E.O. v. AfDB, (2016)* at paras 159, 160.
[19] See footnote 11, supra, EO *v. AfDB*, Decision 96, at para 79.
[20] See footnote 12, supra, *J.O.L. v. AfDB*, AfDBAT Decision 150 (2020).

of probabilities,"[21] and concluded that the charges against the Applicant ***had not*** been established by the administrative record of evidence adduced.

It ordered the proposed sanctions rescinded and the Applicant reinstated to her previous managerial position, grade, and salary, with benefits from the date of her demotion, plus attorneys' fees.

The contrasting outcomes in these two cases aptly reflect the difficult challenges tribunals face in deciding misconduct cases, particularly when nuanced levels of alleged misconduct are present. Such challenges highlight why IATs strive to reach outcomes that are fact-based, law-grounded, well-reasoned, and just, while at the same time respecting their duty to show due deference to the managerial discretion of administrators of international organizations.[22]

The **Commonwealth Secretariat Arbitral Tribunal** (**CSAT**) was established in 1995, and its jurisprudence of reported cases is relatively small, less than 50. Perhaps, for that reason, the author found no cases that expressly involved claims of "*serious misconduct,*" summary dismissal, or other severe sanctions.

Nevertheless, it can perhaps be extrapolated from one CSAT case[23] (albeit a ***non-****disciplinary case*) that this Tribunal may be inclined to apply the "*balance of probabilities*" standard, if called upon to formally adjudicate a serious misconduct disciplinary case. This particular case involved a contested termination of a fixed-term contractor due to poor work performance and poor work attendance. But in deciding that case, the Tribunal made the following revelatory declaration: "***All our findings of fact are made on the balance of probabilities****, having regard to all the material before us.*"[24] [Emphasis added]

Taking that statement at face value, it seems reasonable to assume that the Commonwealth Secretariat Administrative Tribunal may, in due course, expressly affirm its adherence to the "*balance of probabilities*" standard in serious misconduct cases. Accordingly, for current purposes, the CSAT can be provisionally grouped with IAT adherents to the "*balance of probabilities*" test.

Based on the foregoing analysis, one can affirmatively conclude that the "*pre-ponderance of evidence*" ("*balance of probabilities*" or 51%) test is currently being applied in serious misconduct cases by the Administrative Tribunals of: the Asian Development Bank; the Council of Europe; and the African Development Bank. The Commonwealth Secretariat Administrative Tribunal, however, is only provisionally included within this group, pending future, more direct affirmation by that Tribunal's prospective case law.

---

[21] Ibid., at para 86.

[22] For example, compare, *B.L.M. v. AfDB*, AfDBAT Case No. 2007/05 (2008) (dismissal set aside); and *X-D-P v. AfDB*, AfDBAT Judgment No. 81 (2012) (termination for serious misconduct upheld; see paras 88 and 100).

[23] *Kamuganga v. CSAT,* APL/38, 2017.

[24] *Kamuganga v. CSAT,* APL/38, 2017, at para 7.

3 IAT Adherents to the "Substantial Evidence" Test

The World Bank Administrative Tribunal (WBAT) consistently applies the "*substantial evidence*" test when reviewing cases of serious misconduct. Opinions of legal experts about the conceptual definition of "*substantial evidence*" will naturally vary and also opinions about the quantum of evidence needed to meet that threshold. For its part, the World Bank Tribunal prefers the "*substantial evidence*" test because it establishes a higher and a more demanding threshold than the "*preponderance*" or "*balance of probabilities*" or 51% tests. I concur.

Two quite recent World Bank Tribunal cases clearly reflect this view, *Decision 646 (FU)*[25] and *Decision 665 (GK).*[26] In *Decision 646,* the staff member sought to challenge a finding that he had committed serious misconduct by: **(a)** persistent misuse of Bank funds for his travels to Santo Domingo, Dominican Republic and **(b)** fraudulently claiming reimbursement for false hotel expenses.

In its decision, the Tribunal recalled that it "*has held that the burden of proof in misconduct cases lies with the Organization. See, e.g., Dambita, Decision No. 243 [2001], para. 21... [and] has also clearly stipulated on multiple occasions that there must be 'substantial evidence' to support the finding of facts which amount to misconduct... In other words, 'the standard of evidence in disciplinary proceedings leading [...] to misconduct and disciplinary sanctions must be higher than a mere balance of probabilities'.*" [Emphasis added][27]

Applying this standard to the facts of the *FU* case, the Tribunal found that, "*In view of the Applicant's admissions, in addition to the strong and well-developed evidentiary record consisting of compelling and robust testimonial and documentary materials, the Tribunal is satisfied that the Bank has met its burden of proof and that there is substantial evidence, 'higher than a mere balance of probabilities', to support a finding of misconduct in violation of* [the internal law provisions cited]."[28] [Emphasis added]

In WBAT *Decision 665,*[29] an Adviser to the Bank's Executive Director was accused of serious misconduct by impeding, and failing to cooperate with, the Bank's investigation into whether he had concealed important personal financial business interests that he and several family members had in a consultancy firm that held lucrative contracts with the Bank. The administrative sanctions imposed were quite severe: (i) termination; (ii) ineligibility for future World Bank Group (WBG) employment; (iii) restricted access to all WBG premises; and (iv) a permanent written censure in his personnel file.

---

[25] *FU v. International Bank for Reconstruction and Development, WBAT (2021).*

[26] *GK v. The World Bank Group, WBAT (2021).*

[27] *FU*, WBAT at para 98.

[28] *FU*, Decision 646, at para 122.

[29] See footnote 26, supra, *GK v. The World Bank Group, WBAT (2021).*

The Tribunal found that, "*Considering the totality of [the Applicant's] conduct, ... there is substantial evidence to establish that*" the Bank had met the requisite evidentiary threshold to justify dismissal of the complaint.[30] [Emphasis added]

4 IAT Adherent to the "Established and Substantiated" Test

The **NATO Administrative Tribunal** has adopted and routinely applied the "*established and substantiated*" test (which it uses interchangeably with the reverse phrase "*substantiated and established*") in "serious misconduct" cases that involve staff terminations. Analytically speaking, the NATO Tribunal's standard of proof is clearly higher than the "*preponderance*" or "*probabilities*" test, much like the World Bank Tribunal's "*substantial evidence*" test.

BT v. NATO Support and Procurement Agency[31] is a recent NATO serious misconduct case where the "*established and substantiated*" test was applied. There, the appellant was accused of, and a Disciplinary Board (DB) found him guilty of, falsifying a doctor's certificate to justify one day of alleged sick leave. The DB recommended "*the strongest punishment under the [personnel regulations], i.e., dismissal of appellant.*"[32] The NATO General Manager agreed, concluding that the alleged facts were "*substantiated and established.*"[33]

Upon review, the Tribunal affirmed that "*the facts are 'established and substantiated'*"[34] in accordance with "*the requisite legal standard ... that appellant falsified a medical certificate and that appellant's justifications cannot establish any mitigating circumstances.*"[35] [Emphasis added]

The NATO Tribunal also applied this standard in another serious misconduct case (*FB*) handed down in 2021.[36] There, the appellant faced dismissal for allegedly seeking to direct a contract to a particular buyer in the Afghanistan war zone as part of an alleged kickback scheme. A preliminary investigation found that the appellant "*might have been involved*" in such misconduct (see para 7 of the decision). The General Manager (GM) of that NATO Agency concluded that the facts justified the appellant's immediate suspension, pending a Disciplinary Board (DB) review of the accusation. The Board recommended dismissal and the GM ordered its prompt execution. The Appellant then sought tribunal review.

The NATO Tribunal acknowledged at the outset of its decision that, "*the legality of any disciplinary sanction requires that the veracity of the facts of which the*

[30] WBAT Decision 665, *GK v. World Bank Group*, 2021, at p. 42, para 128.

[31] NATO Administrative Tribunal Judgment 1286 (2020).

[32] Ibid., at para 19.

[33] Ibid., at para 21.

[34] Ibid., at paras 75, 77, and 80, p. 16.

[35] Ibid., at para 83.

[36] NATO AT Judgment 1322, *FP v. NATO Support and Procurement Agency* (2021).

person concerned is charged be established."[37] The Tribunal found that each one of the dispositive facts at issue had been "*established*" by the respondent Agency[38] and therefore upheld the sanction and dismissed the complaint. Curiously, the Tribunal gave short shrift to the proportionality of the sanction imposed.

Contrast the outcome of the *FB* decision with that in a 2015 NATO Tribunal decision (*SG*), Judgment 1031.[39] The appellant there was accused of having violated his duties as the Cyber Systems Security Administrator by having illegally accessed his supervisor's mailbox. The Disciplinary Board recommended the appellant's immediate termination, and the Head of that NATO organ concurred.

The Tribunal, however, was not persuaded, and opined as follows, "*The Tribunal considers that the existence of the traces of the above-mentioned documents (see paragraph 21) as such could not lead to the conclusion that appellant had access to his superior's mailbox. Indeed, the factual elements on which the disciplinary findings are based must not be presumed.*"[40]

The Tribunal then held that "*Given the seriousness of the alleged facts and the consequences that may arise from a disciplinary decision based on appellant's breach of confidence, the alleged facts cannot be presumed and the administration must demonstrate the alleged contentions clearly, efficiently, and indisputably in order for the Disciplinary Board to recommend the appropriate sanction.*"[41] The Tribunal found that these criteria had not been established and substantiated by the facts adduced in that case.

Query: Does the more lenient outcome of this 2015 decision suggest that the current NATO Tribunal is applying the "*established and substantiated*" test more stringently than before and more focused on the related issue of proportionality?

5 IAT Adherents to the "Clear and Convincing Evidence" Test

Perhaps the landmark decision in *Molari v. Secretary-General*,[42] handed down in 2011 by the **UN Appeals Tribunal (UNAT),**[43] is one of the clearest illustrations of how contemporary IAT practice seems to be evolving with respect to standards of

[37] Ibid., at para 47.

[38] Ibid., at paras 51 and 52.

[39] *SG v. NATO Communications and Information Agency* (NCIA), Judgment 1031 (2015).

[40] Ibid., at para 79.

[41] Ibid., at para 81.

[42] *Molari v. Secretary-General*, UNAT Judgment 164 (2011). See, also, *Negussie v. UN SG*, UNAT Judgment 700 (2016) (physical assault upon another employee; case remanded to UNDT for further review) and *Aghadiuno v. UN SG*, UNAT Judgment 811 (2018) (fraud, forgery, uttering falsified documents; employee's dismissal upheld).

[43] The former "*UN Administrative Tribunal*" was abolished in December 2009 and was immediately replaced with a new, two-tier system of judicial review comprising a tribunal of first instance, i.e., the "*UN Dispute Tribunal*" (*UNDT*), and one of appellate instance, i.e., the "*UN Appeals Tribunal (UNAT).*"

proof being applied to cases of serious misconduct. The Appeals Tribunal created new precedent when it held that the "*clear and convincing evidence*" standard will henceforth be applied to all serious misconduct cases, particularly where termination of employment is at stake. That holding is by implication also binding upon the first instance **UN Dispute Tribunal (UNDT).** So, both UN tribunals now adhere to this higher standard of proof.

Before the *Molari* decision, the standard of proof applied in UN misconduct cases was "*whether the facts on which the sanction is based have been established,*"[44] (a standard similar to both the World Bank Tribunal's "*substantial evidence*" test and the NATO Tribunal's "*established and substantiated*" test).[45]

Interestingly, the underlying serious misconduct facts in the *Molari* case were strikingly bizarre, self-incriminating, and borderline comic. The Applicant was employed at a UN project based in Copenhagen, Denmark. Relying upon her diplomatic status and immunity from local sales taxes, she sought reimbursement for certain VAT taxes that she had paid. The receipts she submitted for tax reimbursement purposes revealed household purchases that included, *inter alia*, grocery items as milk, fruit, vegetables, and bread, bought between August 2007 and February 2008.

A preliminary administrative review, however, found the timing and volume of those purchases to be "very unusual." For instance, 13 were made on the same day at the same supermarket, using 13 different credit or debit cards. Yet, Ms. Molari repeatedly denied requests for access to her bank statements to audit those purchases.

An expanded investigation found that she had also made 42 purchases on seven different days at two local supermarkets, using nine different bank cards on a single day to buy a total of 19 liters of milk with different levels of fat content. Despite these revelations, Ms. Molari steadfastly continued not cooperating with investigators. Her Executive Director therefore concluded there was sufficient evidence to order her summary dismissal, but he decided to first submit the matter to review by the Disciplinary Committee ("DC").

That Committee concluded: (1) that she should have been summarily dismissed *without prior referral to the DC*; (2) that there was prima facie evidence to find her guilty of fraudulently submitting store receipts for VAT reimbursement; and (3) that she should be terminated with one month's notice and indemnity.

In 2009, Ms. Molari petitioned the newly established UN Dispute Tribunal of first instance to overturn her dismissal, asserting that the legal standard that should have

[44] *Haniya v. UNWRA*, UNAT Judgment 024, para 31 (2010). This case was initially filed at the now-defunct UN Administrative Tribunal in 2006 but was transferred to the UN Appeals Tribunal (UNAT) in 2009 when the former Administrative Tribunal was abolished.

[45] For all other categories of cases that arise before the UN Tribunals, including serious misconduct cases that ***do not*** involve dismissal or termination, the "*preponderance of evidence*" standard continues to be applied by the "*UN Dispute Tribunal*" and the "*UN Appeals Tribunal.*" See 2021 UN Jurisprudence Database, referring to *Iyad Youssef Zaqout v. SG*, UNAT Decision 1183 (2021). Also, see former UN Administrative Tribunal Judgment 941, *Kiwanuka* (1999) and UNDT Judgment 067, *Borhom v. Secretary-General United Nations* (2011).

been applied was "*proof beyond a reasonable doubt,*" not the "*sufficient evidence*" standard the Disciplinary Committee had applied. Her claim that only a reasonable inference that misconduct had occurred was denied.[46] So, in 2010, she appealed to the UN Appeals Tribunal that had just become available to her under the UN's new two-tier system.

The Appeals Tribunal's decision was succinct (9 pages), compelling, and historic. On the merits, it declared that:

> In Ms. Molari's case the facts are so clear as to be irrefutable. No matter what the standard, the Administration has met the burden. **Who buys 19 litres of milk from seven different brands containing four different levels of fat content in one day with nine different bank cards?** [Bolding and italics in the original text].

In view of the parties' dispute as to the appropriate standard of proof, the UN Appeals Tribunal decided to use the *Molari* case to definitively resolve that issue.

In a full-throated ruling, the Appeals Tribunal announced a new UN Tribunals evidentiary standard to be applied henceforth to serious misconduct cases:

> We will not follow the ILOAT in holding that the standard of proof in disciplinary cases is beyond a reasonable doubt. While it is correct that beyond a reasonable doubt is the standard at the ILOAT, this has never been the standard at the United Nations. In disciplinary cases we have required that when a disciplinary sanction is imposed by the Administration, 'the role of the Tribunal is to examine whether the facts on which the sanction is based have been established, whether the established facts qualify as misconduct, and whether the sanction is proportionate to the offence.' (Citing its decision in *Masri v. Secretary-General of the United Nations*, Judgment No. 2010-UNAT-098). **But we have not yet set an exact standard for the quantum of proof required**. [Emphasis added]
>
> Disciplinary cases are not criminal. Liberty is not at stake. But when termination might be the result, we should require sufficient proof. We hold that, *when termination is a possible outcome, misconduct must be established by clear and convincing evidence. Clear and convincing proof requires more than a preponderance of the evidence but less than proof beyond a reasonable doubt*—it means that the truth of the facts asserted is highly probable.[47] [Emphasis added]

The *Molari* decision marks a significant milestone along the continuum of evolving IAT practice with regard to identifying an appropriate standard of proof applicable to cases of serious misconduct. The following two examples reflect this trend.

---

[46] *Molari*, supra, at para 25.

[47] *Molari v. Secretary-General*, UNAT Judgment 164, paras 29–30 (2011). Recent cases typifying how *Molari* has since been applied under the UN's new internal justice system include: *Phillip van de Graaf*, UNDT Judgment 037 (2022), paras 77, 122–123 (verbal and physical altercation with members of the public and suborning perjury to obstruct investigation); *Mubashara Iram*, UNDT Judgment 039 (2022), para 55 (workplace harassment, offensive language, bullying, and intimidation); and *Samuel Bwalya* UNDT Judgment 041 (2022) (forgery and fraud).

The **UNRWA Dispute Tribunal** adjudicates employee disputes arising from the UN Relief and Works Agency for Palestinian Refugees in the Near East.[48] In 2021, the UNRWA Tribunal reviewed a serious misconduct case in which the Applicant had allegedly engaged in sexual exploitation and abuse ("SEA") involving an eighth-grade student at a local school in Jordan as well as another eighth-grade student during the previous academic year.[49] It was further alleged that the Applicant had provided one of the students with a cell phone that contained pornographic content. After an in-depth investigation, UNRWA's Commissioner General imposed summary dismissal upon the Applicant, who then sought judicial review.

In an impressively analyzed and well-reasoned judgment, that Tribunal marshaled the complex factual allegations and upheld the summary dismissal, relying upon the UN Appeals Tribunal "*clear and convincing evidence*" ("*Molari*") standard.[50] The Tribunal enumerated a list of 10 compelling factual considerations that had informed its reasoning and concluded that "*taken cumulatively*," they were sufficient to "*constitute a clear and convincing concatenation of evidence establishing, with a high degree of probability, that the alleged misconduct had, in fact, occurred.*"[51]

The UNRWA Tribunal further held:

> The Tribunal is cognisant of the UNAT's jurisprudence that 'only substantial procedural irregularities will render a disciplinary measure unlawful' and that '[e]ven a very severe disciplinary measure like separation from service can be regarded as lawful if, despite some procedural irregularities, there is clear and convincing evidence of grave misconduct, especially if the misconduct consists of a physical or sexual assault' (*Sall* 2018-UNAT-889, para 33). Accordingly, the Tribunal holds that, in the present case, these [procedural] mistakes are not significant enough to render unlawful the imposition of the disciplinary measure of summary dismissal.[52]

6 The Administrative Tribunal of the Organization of American States (OASAT)

OASAT is one of the most recent tribunals to adopt the Molari "*clear and convincing evidence*" standard for disciplinary cases that involve serious misconduct where summary dismissal or employment termination is the recommended sanction.

[48] It should be noted that this Tribunal, established in 2010, is one of the most recent to join the community of International Administrative Tribunals. It became operational in June 2011.

[49] *Mohammad v. Commissioner of UNRWA*, UNRWA/DT, Judgment 003 (2021).

[50] See the UNRWA Tribunal's reference to the UNAT's decision in *Negussie*, UNAT Judgment 700 (2016), quoting para 18 thereof ("*[W]hen termination is a possible outcome, misconduct must be established by clear and convincing evidence,*" which "*means that the truth of the facts asserted is highly probable*").

[51] *Mohammad* (supra, footnote 49), at para 69.

[52] Ibid., at para 45.

Adoption of this new standard of proof for the OAS was announced in Judgment 169 (*Griner*) (2022).[53]

A majority of the OAS Tribunal judges decided to take this significant step, motivated primarily by two compelling considerations:

(i) the disturbing facts in that case revealed a manifestly flawed administrative investigation that the chief investigator sought to normalize and defend; and,
(ii) this case was apparently the first instance in the Tribunal's extensive jurisprudence in which it faced a need to give heightened scrutiny to the propriety and fairness of continued reliance upon the traditional "*preponderance of evidence*" standard in cases that involve serious misconduct including a summary dismissal disciplinary sanction.

In reaching its decision, the OAS Tribunal majority felt it could not simply ignore the following set of disturbing considerations:

(a) the seriously flawed process by which the OAS Inspector General (OIG) conducted what clearly amounted to an incomplete investigation;
(b) the manifestly weak OIG investigative report in which the OIG relied heavily upon triple hearsay statements to support a dubious "*serious misconduct*" finding;
(c) the report's disproportionate recommendation of "*summary dismissal*," the most severe sanction possible, despite the glaringly weak facts of this case;
(d) the Secretary-General's apparently unquestioned acceptance of the OIG's recommendation;
(e) the OIG's ***and*** the SG's surprising indifference when presented with proof from a key witness that incriminating hearsay statements attributed to her in the report were false, fabricated, and pointedly "disavowed"[54] in writing by her;
(f) the OIG's acknowledgment at the hearing that he never bothered to interview that witness, yet attributed to her triple hearsay statements that he heavily relied upon as bedrock evidence that the Complainant was indeed guilty of serious misconduct.

Accordingly, in view of those foregoing considerations, the Tribunal majority concluded that justice in this case demanded the landmark ruling it handed down in the following terms:

> 151. "The Tribunal appreciates that cases of 'misconduct', even 'serious misconduct', will inevitably arise from time to time and will definitely warrant thorough OIG investigation. However, the OIG's conduct of *this* investigation has highlighted for the Tribunal the need to

[53] OASAT, Judgment 169, *Griner v. Secretary-General* (decided en banc by a 4–2, majority) (2022). **Full Disclosure**: The author of this article was the first opining judge and the principal author of the *Griner* Judgment.

[54] *Griner*, OASAT, Judgment 169, ibid., at para 45, at p. 14.

give heightened scrutiny to what should be the appropriate standard of proof when serious misconduct is alleged and there is the possibility of summary dismissal or termination from employment.

152. The Tribunal is aware that for a number of decades at some other international administrative tribunals the 'preponderance of evidence' standard has been routinely applied in misconduct cases. Indeed, it appears that has been the prevailing standard of proof used by this Organization's Office of the Inspector General since its establishment. OAS internal law does not expressly prescribe or proscribe its use. Rather, we presume the OIG simply conformed its practice to that of its counterpart offices at other international organizations, in line with the Uniform Guidelines for OIG Investigations. [Footnote omitted].

153. However, the Tribunal has observed that the 'preponderance' standard is no longer applied universally at all international administrative tribunals, and that, in recent years, some tribunals have evolved away from that standard and have begun to apply other standards, especially in cases of serious misconduct... This growing divergence in tribunal practice suggests that some have concluded that, in serious misconduct cases and particularly where severe sanctions may be imposed, due process demands a higher standard of proof of alleged wrong-doing than the customary 'preponderance' standard.

154. In 2011, the UN Appeals Tribunal handed down a seminal opinion, *Molari vs. United Nations Secretary-General*, setting forth its view of the appropriate standard of proof that the UN Tribunal will apply in reviewing disciplinary cases that involve the possibility of an employee's separation from service ... [and it opined as follows:]

'Disciplinary cases are not criminal. Liberty is not at stake. But when termination might be the result, we should require sufficient proof. **We hold that, when termination is a possible outcome, misconduct must be established by clear and convincing evidence. Clear and convincing proof requires more than a preponderance of the evidence** but less than proof beyond a reasonable doubt—it means that the truth of the facts asserted is highly probable'. [Emphasis added and footnote omitted] [...]

156. We find the UNAT's reasoning and holdings in *Molari* to be persuasive. As explained at length above, the deficient conduct and outcomes of the OIG investigation caused the Tribunal to give heightened scrutiny and deliberation to the issue of the appropriate standard of proof to apply in cases of serious misconduct, particularly when there is the possibility of summary dismissal or other form of termination.

157. After internal debate and due consideration, we hold that, henceforth, in serious misconduct cases, this Tribunal will be prepared to affirm such a finding and a sanction of corresponding gravity, provided that serious misconduct has been proved by 'clear and convincing evidence'. Moreover, we hold that the application of this standard of proof is consonant with 'the basic principles' set forth in Article I of the Tribunal's Statute, as well as with universally-established norms of fairness and due process widely recognized within the international community of administrative tribunals."[55]

The Tribunal thus ordered monetary relief (including legal fees); Complainant's reinstatement; and immediate expungement from his personnel records of the finding of "*serious misconduct*" and the recommended "summary dismissal."

[55] OASAT Judgment 169, *Griner v. SG*, at pp. 47–48.

7 IAT Adherents to the "Beyond a Reasonable Doubt" Standard

In a 2022 case,[56] the **International Labor Organization Tribunal (ILOAT)**, re-affirmed its "outlier" status within the community of IATs as the only tribunal that adheres to "*beyond a reasonable doubt*" as the appropriate standard of proof in cases of serious misconduct.[57] The misconduct alleged in that case was the wrongful receipt of family allowance benefits based upon a fraudulent claim of "single-parent" status. The recommended administrative sanction was dismissal.

On the applicable standard of proof, the ILO Tribunal noted that:

> The case law of the Tribunal is clear where [fraud] is involved [. . .] the burden of proof [. . .] of misconduct falls on the organization and *it must be proved beyond a reasonable doubt* (see, for example, Judgment 4364, consideration 10). In reviewing a decision to sanction a staff member for misconduct, the Tribunal will not ordinarily engage in the determination of whether the burden of proof has been met but rather will assess whether a finding of guilt beyond reasonable doubt could properly have been made (see, for example, Judgment 4362, considerations 7 to 10).

The Tribunal held that it was "*satisfied a finding of guilt beyond reasonable doubt of the charge alleged could not properly have been made.*" Accordingly, it set aside the decision to terminate the complainant's employment and ordered her reinstatement.

At publication, the author's review of decisions posted in the ILOAT's database between 2010 and 2022 indicated that this Tribunal had decided only five other serious misconduct cases that involved the sanction of dismissal. A review of those cases indicates that, with only one exception, the respondent international organization's finding of serious misconduct was set aside by the ILO Tribunal for failing to satisfy the "*beyond a reasonable doubt*" standard.[58]

Against this track record of ILOAT decision-making in serious misconduct cases, a question that naturally arises is, "*Why do more than 5 dozen international organizations still recognize the ILOAT's jurisdiction instead of accepting that of*

---

[56] ILOAT Judgment 4491, (*L-B v. European Patent Office, EPO*), at consideration 19 (2022).

[57] Although the ILOAT is the sole adherent to this standard, it is curious that, at present, the ILOAT has jurisdiction to review labor disputes arising from *no less than 58* international organizations; more than any other IAT.

[58] The sole case found where the dismissal of the complaint was upheld is ILOAT Judgment 3295, *R.D.A.G. v. Pan American Health Organization,* (PAHO) (2014). The four cases where serious misconduct findings were "set aside" are: Judgment 4047, *H. (No. 24) v. European Patent Office* (EPO) (2018); Judgment 3848, *D. v. Int'l Organization for Migration* (IOM) (2017); Judgment 3083, *C.U. v. UN Industrial Development Organization* (UNIDO) (2012); and Judgment 2892, *P. G.T. v. International Telecommunication Union* (ITO) (2010). Absent a comprehensive review of all ILOAT cases spanning more years, these case results should be seen as only indicative of *recent outcomes* and not necessarily representative of a wider pool of ILOAT cases that could reveal different outcomes.

another IAT, for instance, the UN Tribunal system, where 'clear and convincing evidence' would be an easier standard to prove in such cases?"

A related question is "*Are many of the ILOAT's constituent International Organizations discouraged from even initiating serious misconduct administrative proceedings against personnel whose misconduct credibly deserves dismissal or other severe sanctions, due to the perceived impossibility of withstanding the ILOAT's 'beyond a reasonable doubt' scrutiny, on appeal?*"

To date, only two international organizations (IOs) have withdrawn from the ILOAT's jurisdiction, both for reasons unrelated to serious misconduct cases.[59] Perhaps, in time, other ILOAT member IOs will migrate to another IAT expressly to enjoy a less draconian threshold of proof in serious misconduct cases.

8 To Strike a Fair Balance Between the Staff's vs. the Institution's Interests

This article began by highlighting two interrelated points. One, the inherently defamatory nature of serious misconduct accusations and their potential for devastating career consequences for the employee concerned. Two, tribunals are naturally inclined to devote close scrutiny to the overall quality of the administrative proceedings when such accusations are administratively upheld and when summary dismissal or other severe sanctions are imposed.

At the same time, however, tribunals recognize that they have a corresponding *duty* to show proper deference to the institution's inherent managerial prerogatives, including its authority to lawfully discipline wrong-doing by staff and to impose proportional sanctions, without fear of undue judicial oversight or intrusion.

These competing interests sometimes require IATs to take due account of the primary substantive mission, or *raison d'être,* of a given international organization when adjudicating cases of serious misconduct. In such instances, the judicial challenge is to strike the right balance between ensuring respect for the accused civil servant's due process rights as well as the rights and equities of the institution in question.

An excellent example of this balancing challenge is illustrated in a recent serious misconduct case decided by the World Bank Administrative Tribunal, *GK v. WBG*, WBAT, Decision 665 (2021), also discussed above.[60] There, the Tribunal eloquently and appropriately addressed the importance of this balancing process, by linking it to the underlying facts and the World Bank Group's core mission:

---

[59] In 2016, the Permanent Court of Arbitration withdrew from ILOAT, after deciding to start resolving its employment disputes through final, binding arbitration under UNCITRAL Arbitration Rules. In 2017, the Centre for the Development of Entreprise (CDE) discontinued recognition of ILOAT jurisdiction because CDE was shuttering its operations.

[60] See footnote 26, supra, and its accompanying text where this case is summarized.

141. With regard to the interests of the Bank Group, the Tribunal notes the Bank's contention that the Applicant's noncooperation was particularly serious as it 'hindered INT's ability to investigate serious allegations of fraud and corruption: misconduct that the Tribunal itself has found to be one of the most serious forms of misconduct as it poses significant financial and reputational risk to the institution'. The Bank explains: Allowing a staff member to deliberately hinder an investigation would render the institution powerless in its efforts to combat fraud and corruption in its operations. Not only is it understandable for an HRVP [Human Resources Vice President] to impose severe sanctions for fraud and corruption, but it is equally understandable to impose severe sanctions for conduct that would frustrate the institution's ability to reliably identify and address fraud and corruption committed by its staff. Indeed, without means for enforcement and deterrence, there would be no accountability, jeopardizing the integrity and reputation of the institution, as allegations of misconduct would go substantially uninvestigated and unsanctioned.

142. In *FU*, Decision No. 646 [2021], para. 156, the Tribunal stated: It is the Bank's duty to investigate all forms of misconduct. *Moreover, the WBG endeavors to be a leader in international efforts to eliminate corruption and to improve governance. Where financial discrepancies or irregularities are suspected or identified in any part of the Bank's workforce, it is incumbent on the Bank,* in pursuit of its commitment to integrity and its promotion of the highest standards by staff members in the performance of their duties, *to investigate such discrepancies and irregularities* and to be satisfied that any such discrepancies and/or irregularities have been fully accounted for and satisfactorily explained. It cannot 'turn a blind eye' to such matters.

143. *Considering this, the Tribunal is fully cognizant of the Bank's interest in preserving its integrity as an institution* and upholding its impartiality in client relations – goals which may be undermined if staff members are able to frustrate investigations into serious misconduct allegations through their noncooperation. *It is therefore understandable that the HRVP may wish to seriously sanction conduct which could undermine those goals.*[61] (Decision 665, pp. 46–47, paras 141–143.) [Emphasis added]

9 What Provisional Conclusions Can be Drawn from this Snapshot Survey?

From the foregoing discussion, the following conclusions seem beyond dispute:

(**A**) International Administrative Tribunals (IATs) are currently using multiple (at least eight) different standards of proof in cases of serious misconduct involving imposition of severe sanctions.

These divergent standards or tests include the following:

- ample evidence (UN Tribunal pre-2011);[62]
- cogent evidence (UN Tribunal pre-2011);[63]
- preponderance of the evidence/balance of probabilities/51% test;
- credible and convincing evidence;
- substantial evidence;

[61] WBAT Decision 665, *GK v. WBG*, pp. 46–47, paras 141–143 (2021).

[62] See, e.g., Former UN Administrative Tribunal, Judgment No. 897, *Jhuthi v.SG*, at p. 14 (1998).

[63] Former UN Administrative Tribunal, Judgment No. 928, *Abdulhati, et al. v. UNWRA*, at pp. 18–20 (1999).

- established and substantiated/substantiated and established evidence;
- clear and convincing evidence;
- beyond a reasonable doubt.

(**B**) Definitions of these standards of proof are not always clear-cut. Indeed, some standards seem closely analogous, and even to overlap conceptually with others.

(**C**) Tribunal judgments do not always expressly identify *by name* which exact standard was applied in a given case. Sometimes tribunals simply choose to uphold or set aside an impugned administrative decision, based upon an overall assessment of the totality of the evidence and circumstances involved.

(D) At some international organizations (like the Asian Development Bank), the applicable standard of proof may even be predetermined as a matter of institutional policy, enshrined in governing staff rules. This uncommon practice seems fundamentally at odds with what should normally be a Tribunal's inherent judicial discretion to determine, as necessary, the most appropriate standard of proof to apply.

9.1 "Serious" vs. "Lesser" (or "More Routine") Misconduct

In reviewing the foregoing cases that provided the grist for this analysis, it did not go unnoticed that, for some international organizations and their tribunals, certain acts of staff misconduct appear to be viewed with a darker jaundiced eye, and thus labeled as "serious misconduct" and punished accordingly, whereas at other institutions the same or comparable acts may not be.

Query: Should such disparate views by international organizations and tribunals of what constitutes "serious misconduct" and appropriate disciplinary sanctions be considered as an immaterial quirk of practice? Or, do such disparities beg the question of whether there should be an attempt to categorize what constitutes *"serious" vs. "lesser" (or more routine) misconduct* and their appropriate corresponding sanctions?

For example, recall the NATO Administrative Tribunal Judgment 1286 (2020), *BT v. NATO Support and Procurement Agency* (see footnote 31, supra). It involved an employee's dismissal due to a single, *first-time incident* of falsifying a medical leave claim to cover a portion of only one day of leave. Notably, both the NATO Agency and the NATO Tribunal considered that falsification sufficiently grave to justify outright dismissal of that employee instead of a lesser sanction for a first offense.

Similarly, in the recent OAS Tribunal case alluded to above *(Griner)*,[64] an employee of 26 years with an otherwise unblemished personnel record was accused of orchestrating/assisting a disinformation campaign that adversely affected a joint

[64]OAS AT, Judgment 169; see footnote 53, supra.

visit to Honduras by the OAS Chief of Staff and a Member State ambassador. The proposed sanction was summary dismissal and a reduced pension.

Query: Did these two types of misconduct merit the highest sanction—dismissal—or a lesser one more calibrated to the totality of their circumstances?[65]

Such queries are fodder for interesting future deliberations among IAT judges. In that regard, it bears noting that the United Nations has already contributed some useful consideration to this issue, as reflected in two charts published on its IOIS website. These charts respectively list examples of categories of misconduct that fall within either "***Category I—Serious Misconduct***" or "***Category II—Routine Misconduct.***" The first chart lists eleven examples of acts that typically should be investigated and sanctioned as "*serious misconduct*" and the second offers a shorter list of acts to be investigated and sanctioned as "*routine misconduct.*" To be sure, these charts do not purport to enumerate all potential forms or levels of misconduct imaginable, but they do merit review for discussion purposes.[66]

For convenient reference, a copy of the UN's "Misconduct Charts" is attached to this chapter as Annex I. But these charts can also be found online at the UN Investigations Manual (2015) website (at pp. 8–9) (https://oios.un.org/sites/oios.un.org/files/general/investigations_manual.pdf).

10 Closing Observations

The central focus of this article has been to survey, identify, and compare varying standards of proof that IATs are currently applying in reviewing cases of serious misconduct where severe sanctions, such as dismissal, are at stake. From this group of 11 international administrative tribunals—that are part of an IAT universe that continues to *expand*[67]—we conclude that at present there is ***no*** common or even majoritarian standard of proof being applied among those IATs. Rather, the recent landscape of IAT practice reflects both continued divergence but also evolution in standards of proof being applied to this special class of disputes.

For the author, it will be interesting to learn in time whether any of the current adherents to the preponderance or balance of probabilities tests (or other similar tests mentioned) will adopt a higher standard, as in the UN Appeals Tribunal's *Molari* case ("*clear and convincing evidence*" test) for serious misconduct cases. Will others, like the OAS Tribunal, decide that that standard of proof strikes a fairer balance that

[65] The hierarchy of sanctions commonly applied at IATs can include: a written or oral admonition; a written censure; demotion in managerial status; reduction in salary; suspension with or without pay, inter alia, up to dismissal.

[66] To the best of the author's knowledge, the UN Investigative Office (IOIS) continues to be guided by these charts.

[67] One of the newest tribunals to join the IAT universe is "OFAT," *the Administrative Tribunal of the Organization of Petroleum Exporting Countries' (OPEC) Fund for International Development* established in March 2022. It too will function as a final appellate review body for the resolution of staff-related grievances.

ensures due respect for ***both*** the international civil servant's due process rights ***and*** the legitimate managerial and disciplinary prerogatives of international organizations?

No doubt these and other pertinent questions deserve further reflection. However, this survey suggests that several IATs are gradually moving away from the "*preponderance of evidence*" standard previously entrenched at many institutions. One can ask "why?" A plausible explanation could include the following rationales: (1) over the past several decades, the international stature of IATs has grown, steadily; (2) as IATs have proliferated in number, they have studied, and learned from each other's case law and experiences; (3) they have attracted many highly distinguished jurists as judges;[68] and (4) they have incrementally produced a unique and impressive subset of International Law (Civil Service Law).

In closing, although this survey was admittedly not exhaustive, it seeks to offer instructive insights into the contemporary landscape of IAT practices, with regard to the divergent standards of proof applied in cases of serious misconduct.

So, now seemed as good a time as any to take a "*snapshot*" of that evolving landscape. Its primary stakeholders (IAT judges, scholars, claimants' and defense counsel, and staff associations) will no doubt play leading roles in shaping the future course of that landscape, and the ensuing implications for IATs' practice.

By: Judge (Ret.) T. Michael Peay,

Administrative Tribunal, Organization of American States (OAS)

[68] For instance, former International Court of Justice Judge (and also former ICJ President) Stephen M. Schwebel (1981–2000) later served as President of the Administrative Tribunals of both the IMF (1994–2009) and the World Bank (appointed 2007). Providentially, Professor Schwebel taught the author International Law and International Organizations when he was a student at the Johns Hopkins University, School of Advanced International Studies (SAIS), 1968–1970.

Reasonable Doubt About Proof "Beyond Reasonable Doubt" in International Administrative Law

Kieran Bradley

Contents

1 Introduction 110
2 The ILOAT Foundational Cases 111
2.1 *In Re Pollicino* (1984) and *In Re Navarro* (1989) 111
2.2 *Post*-Navarro *Judgments* 112
2.3 *J.R.D. v. WHO* and *C.C. v. WIPO* (2009) 113
2.4 A Brief Comment on *In re Navarro* 114
3 The *Raison d'etre* and Features of the Standard "Beyond Reasonable Doubt" 114
3.1 "Severity of the Consequences" of a Disciplinary Proceeding 114
3.2 "No Comparison with a Criminal Law Standard of Proof" 116
3.3 The Importance (or Not) of Stating the Standard of Proof 117
4 "Reasonable Doubt" in Contemporary ILOAT Practice 118
4.1 *L.-B. v. EPO*: Home Alone? 118
4.2 Single Parenthood and the Benefits of a "Mistaken" Declaration 120
4.3 A Brief Comment on *L.-B. v. EPO* 120
4.4 How to Dispel "Reasonable Doubt" 122
4.5 Paternal Parenting 122
5 Standard of Proof in Harassment Disputes 123
5.1 Proving Harassment Allegations: "The Further Off from England, the Nearer Is to France" 123
5.2 The Standard of Proof in Disciplinary Proceedings Against an Alleged Harasser ... 124
6 Reactions to the ILOAT's Case Law 126
6.1 Other International Organisations: Not in My Name 126
6.2 The International Labour Organization 127

Kieran Bradley, Judge of the Administrative Tribunals of the IMF and the Inter-American Development Bank Group. All views expressed are entirely provisional and strictly personal, and are presented here exclusively for the purpose of academic debate; they do not prejudice in any way the position the author may take in any other capacity.

K. Bradley (✉)
IMF Administrative Tribunal, Luxembourg, Luxembourg

T. Bravo, K. Bradley (eds.), *Judicial Review in International Administrative Law*, Law for Professionals, https://doi.org/10.1007/978-3-031-71840-3_7

7 *Eppur si muove*: A Shift in the ILOAT Case Law? ... 127
7.1 G.M. v. IAEA ... 127
7.2 Potential Repercussions of *G.M. v. IAEA* ... 129
8 Concluding Remarks ... 131
References ... 133

1 Introduction

The staff of international organisations are in a rather particular legal position compared to employees in the private sector. The organisation is at once a public body established under international law and an employer; its decisions in its latter capacity are generally treated as benefitting from the presumption of regularity which attaches to administrative acts. Thus, for example, in a non-disciplinary context where a decision taken by delegation was challenged, the International Labour Organization Administrative Tribunal ("ILOAT") has held that "the presumption of regularity applies in the absence of cogent evidence to the contrary."[1] Similarly, the United Nations Appeals Tribunal ("UNAT") has relied on an "evidential presumption of validity (*omnia praesumuntur rite esse acta*) which assumes that administrative and quasi-judicial decisions are in compliance with the principle of legality until determined otherwise."[2]

The application of such a presumption in a disciplinary context in an international organisation could be seen as running counter to the presumption of innocence which is universally acknowledged to obtain in the context of criminal proceedings,[3] and arguably should also obtain where the career of a staff member may be terminated by way of a sanction. International administrative tribunals have adopted a variety of standards of proof in disciplinary contexts, primarily either the simple balance of probabilities or the requirement of "clear and convincing evidence." As is well known,[4] alone amongst international administrative tribunals,[5] the ILOAT requires the defendant organisation to justify a finding of misconduct "beyond [a] reasonable doubt."[6]

[1] ILOAT Judgment 2915, *H.L. v. WIPO*, consideration 14.

[2] Judgment No. 2021-UNAT-1148, *Fogarty v. IMO*, consideration 59.

[3] Article 11(1), 1948 Universal Declaration of Human Rights.

[4] See notably, Peay (in press), this volume.

[5] While in *KF v. Commission,* the EU General Court has noted that a defendant institution was able to prove a particular fact "beyond reasonable doubt," it was merely replying to an argument of the applicant to the effect that even if this were the test, it would be satisfied, rather than adopting a radically new standard of proof in staff cases (Case T-415/20, EU:T:2021:368, paras 101 and 103; *contra* Tavadian and Ducamin (2023), pp. 152–153).

[6] Sometimes formulated as "beyond *a* reasonable doubt": the shorter version is preferred throughout the present chapter.

Notwithstanding the ILOAT's status as the most venerable of the international administrative tribunals, whose judgments are often relied upon in argument before other such tribunals, its stance on the standard of proof remains that of an "outlier."[7] In *Molari v. Secretary-General of the United Nations,* the United Nations Appeals Tribunal took the highly unusual step, in the opening paragraphs of a judgment, of explicitly distancing itself from the ILOAT standard of proof in disciplinary cases, and adding:

> [d]isciplinary cases are not criminal. Liberty is not at stake. But when termination might be the result, we should require sufficient proof. We hold that, when termination is a possible outcome, misconduct must be established by clear and convincing evidence [which] means that the truth of the facts asserted is highly probable.[8]

The present chapter traces the origin of this standard of proof in ILOAT case law and examines its application in practice, particularly in the context of disputes regarding allegations of harassment.

2 The ILOAT Foundational Cases

2.1 *In Re Pollicino* (1984) and *In Re Navarro* (1989)

In its 1984 judgment in *In re Pollicino*, where a disciplinary sanction had been challenged, the Tribunal held that once the staff member had denied the misconduct, the burden of proof shifted to the organisation. In such circumstances, "[t]he Tribunal will not require absolute proof, which is almost impossible to provide on such a matter. It will dismiss the complaint if there is a set of precise and concurring presumptions."[9] This is prima facie a lower standard of proof than "beyond reasonable doubt."

The requirement of proof beyond reasonable doubt for disciplinary matters has been traced back to *In re Navarro*.[10] A staff member of the WHO had been accused of typing and sending two memoranda containing, in the Tribunal's words, "language [which] was obviously calculated to intimidate by threats to the life of senior officers of the Organization." It was established that the memoranda had been typed on a particular model of typewriter; an examination of all the typewriter ribbons used in that model threw suspicion on Ms. Navarro. The record of a meeting between her and her line manager, a personnel officer and a third staff member, noted that the accused had confessed to the deed and invited her to acknowledge the truth of the charges. However, Ms. Navarro subsequently denied having typed the memoranda and contended that any statement she had made at the meeting had been made under

[7] Peay, *op. cit.*, citing OASAT Judgment 169, *Griner v. SG,* pp. 47 and 48.

[8] Judgment 2011-UNAT-164, paras 1 and 2.

[9] *In re Pollicino*, Judgment 635.

[10] ILOAT Judgment No. 969.

duress. At the same time, she sought to justify the content of the memoranda as "mere expressions of protest" and as reflecting "widespread dissatisfaction in the ranks," and refused to provide her own version of the meeting.[11] On the grounds that "the Organization could only infer that [Ms Navarro] had typed the two memoranda," the personnel officer summarily dismissed her for serious misconduct. The Regional Board of Appeal upheld the personnel officer's decision, while the headquarters Board of Appeal was unable to come to a decision on the accused's appeal.

It appears from the text of the Judgment that the Director-General

> informed [Ms Navarro] that he was *satisfied beyond any reasonable doubt* that she had been at least 'involved in the preparation of the memoranda' and 'aware of the use of [her] typewriter for that purpose' and, in the absence of explanation from her, that she had actually typed them; he rejected her appeal (emphasis added).[12]

The Tribunal ruled as follows:

> [i]t is common ground that the burden of proof rests on the Organization. By declining to admit the charges, as she was entitled to do, [Ms Navarro] required the Organization to prove its case; and although the proceedings are not criminal the seriousness of the charges and the concomitant penalty demand that before there can be a finding against [her] the charges must be proved beyond reasonable doubt.[13]

The Tribunal took the view that "there is no doubt whatever that the memoranda were typed on the [Ms Navarro's] typewriter" and concluded that "the presumption arises, in the absence of any evidence to the contrary, that the memoranda . . . were typed by her."[14] Her appeal was thus rejected.

2.2 *Post*-Navarro *Judgments*

In its 1995 judgment in *In re Wadie*, where the defendant organisation was once again the WHO, the Tribunal indicated that it would apply the *Pollicino* standard of "precise and concurring presumptions."[15]

In *D.A.D. v. WIPO* (2006), the complainant alleged, inter alia, that the offensive matter that had appeared on his computer had been placed there by means of unsolicited email. The Tribunal accepted, "despite the uncertainty that remains as to whether unsolicited messages appeared on the [complainant's] hard disk, the

[11] The accused person appears to have been particularly poorly represented, if at all; attempting to justify the content of the offending memoranda while denying any participation in their production was hardly a convincing indication of her innocence.

[12] Ibid., last paragraph, p. 1.

[13] Ibid., consideration 16.

[14] Ibid., consideration 18.

[15] *In re Wadie*, Judgment 1384, consideration 10.

defendant ... [had] proved the fact on which the charges ... [we]re based and established that they were indeed such as to justify his dismissal."[16]

In *I. L. v. WHO* (2008) on the other hand, the Tribunal once again reverted to the requirement of proof beyond reasonable doubt.[17]

It seems that, at this point in time, the Tribunal's views regarding the general standard of proof in disciplinary matters were not entirely settled.

2.3 *J.R.D. v. WHO* and *C.C. v. WIPO* (2009)

While the adoption of the higher standard of proof was of no avail to Ms. Navarro, it had a determinative effect in *J.R.D. v. WHO.*[18] In October 2002, J.R.D. had submitted a health insurance claim in respect of the hospitalisation of his son for a hernia operation for nine days the previous August. The Medical Director of "the (sic) New Delhi hospital" refused to respond to the Administration's request for information regarding any medical treatment of J.R.D.'s son. On 2 and 7 January 2003, J.R.D. was asked to bring his son to the Medical Service, which he failed to do; instead, J.R.D. went on sick leave himself until 22 January, finally bringing his son to the Medical Service on 28 January 2003. The Regional Staff Physician concluded that the boy "had indeed undergone surgery but that the surgical wound did not appear to be more than 10 to 14 days old." This conclusion was in effect confirmed by a Consultant Surgeon a few days later. J.R.D. was subsequently dismissed for misconduct for presenting a fraudulent health insurance claim with respect to his son.[19]

In his appeal against that decision, J.R.D. particularly relied on a certificate from the Medical Director of the New Delhi hospital which he had submitted to the Director of Administration and Finance on 22 March 2003, and which attested that a hernia operation had been performed on J.R.D.'s son in August 2002. The Regional Board of Appeal found "no conclusive evidence of the alleged fraud," while the Headquarters Board concluded that "the Administration had failed to prove fraud beyond reasonable doubt." The Director-General nonetheless rejected J.R.D.'s appeal in its entirety and dismissed him from service.

Citing consideration 16 of *In re Navarro*, the Tribunal noted that "when misconduct is denied, it is for the Administration to prove it and prove it beyond reasonable doubt." Here both the organisation's Boards of Appeal disagreed with the dismissal decision; moreover, J.R.D. had produced a certificate showing surgery had been performed on a 14-year-old male in August 2002. The Tribunal observed that the organisation was therefore claiming in effect that J.R.D. had "subjected his son to unnecessary surgery to conceal his fraud" with the complicity of his family and

---

[16] Judgment No. 2555, consideration 13.

[17] Judgment No. 2699, consideration 9.

[18] Judgment No. 2786.

[19] J.R.D. was also accused of defrauding health insurance claim for his wife; this aspect of the case is not further considered.

different medical staff: as surgery had been performed on a young male, "it would have been much easier for [J.R.D.] to produce that person and pass him off as his son than to engage in the elaborate deception asserted." The Tribunal accordingly upheld J.R.D.'s appeal.

In *C.C. v. WIPO*, the defendant organisation argued that "the relevant standard of proof is that of 'precise and concurring presumptions'," as the Tribunal had held in *In re Pollicino*.[20] The Tribunal's answer was that "the finding of serious misconduct appears to have been taken with a complete disregard of the relevant standard of proof," though without specifying in this judgment what the new standard was, or why the *Pollicino* standard had been abandoned.

2.4 A Brief Comment on *In re Navarro*

One might have expected that such a significant step by the ILOAT as embracing a standard of proof not then found elsewhere in international administrative law would have merited a detailed examination of the issue and/or a comprehensive explanation of the reasons for its adoption. If so, one would be disappointed; indeed, it is difficult to avoid the impression that this became the general standard of proof by accident rather than design. It does not appear from the report of *In re Navarro* that the question of the proper standard of proof was the subject of any debate between the parties or extended consideration by the Tribunal. In fact, it was the Director-General of the organisation who introduced the notion of a standard of proof "beyond reasonable doubt" into the proceedings, which was then taken up by the complainant in her arguments before the Tribunal. In finding that "there was adequate evidence upon which the Director-General might properly conclude that [Ms Navarro's guilt] was beyond reasonable doubt," the Tribunal appears to have been merely affirming the validity of the decision at issue in the light of the arguments of the respondent organisation, rather than laying down a universally applicable rule on the standard of proof in disciplinary matters.

Be that as it may, the application of the standard of proof beyond reasonable doubt in disciplinary matters has become an integral part of the ILOAT's case law, not to say its identity.

3 The *Raison d'etre* and Features of the Standard "Beyond Reasonable Doubt"

3.1 "Severity of the Consequences" of a Disciplinary Proceeding

The Tribunal currently justifies the continued application of this standard of proof on the basis that "often disciplinary proceedings can have severe consequences for the affected staff member ... and in these circumstances it is appropriate to require a

[20] Judgment No. 2879, section C, p. 8.

high level of satisfaction on the part of the organization that the disciplinary measure is justified because the misconduct has been proved."[21] This may have been the case in *Navarro*, *J.R.D.* and *C.C.*, but is far from being a feature of all the disciplinary disputes which come before the ILOAT.

Recourse to this standard assumes in effect that all disciplinary charges which may be laid, and all disciplinary penalties which may be imposed, are "serious." In practice, however, the disciplinary sanction is determined at the very end of the proceedings, at a point in time when the disciplinary body has already made its findings of fact, presumptively beyond reasonable doubt. To rely on the "seriousness" of the possible sanction before determining the veracity of the facts and appreciating the character of the alleged behaviour might be seen as contravening the rights of defence of the person concerned. As a result, this standard of proof is in principle required by the ILOAT to be applied to all disciplinary proceedings, even where the originating incident and the concomitant disciplinary measure might be considered comparatively trivial.

Disciplinary proceedings do not always have particularly "severe" consequences, and many disciplinary measures can be expunged from the staff file of the person concerned after a relatively brief period, such as three or five years. In *S. (No. 6) v. WIPO*, for example, the Tribunal held that a decision to delay advancement to the next salary step required proof beyond reasonable doubt, while noting that this was "the second lightest disciplinary measure available to the Organization."[22] Similarly, this standard of proof has been required for the imposition of a decision downgrading the staff member.[23] In each case, the sanction might well have no permanent effect on a staff member's career, providing that this is of sufficient duration subsequent to the imposition of the disciplinary measure to allow its nullification over time. In practice, the impact of a delay in advancement, or even a downgrading, may be completely eradicated by a later promotion. In *S. v. OPCW*, the competent authorities of the organisation were at pains to demonstrate the breach of the staff member's obligation beyond reasonable doubt, even though the offence had attracted a mere written censure; moreover, the staff member had left the organisation before disciplinary proceedings had been initiated and the impact on his career was at best uncertain, possibly nil.[24]

If it is the impact of the organisation's decision on the career of the staff member which is the decisive factor, an argument can be made that the same standard should apply to other situations. Bringing a staff member's career to an end for professional incompetence, issuing them with a negative performance evaluation, or refusing the renewal of their contract are decisions that may have a significantly greater practical and/or psychological impact on the person concerned than the issuing of a written

[21] *O. (No. 2) v. ICC*, Judgment No. 4360.

[22] Judgment No. 4478, considerations 10 and 12.

[23] *L. v. EPO*, Judgment No. 3969.

[24] Judgment No. 4373, consideration 10; that said, it must be recognised that the appellant considered the imposition of the sanction sufficiently serious to take proceedings to challenge it.

warning, yet the organisation need only prove the existence of the underlying facts according to the balance of probabilities to justify these decisions.

3.2 "No Comparison with a Criminal Law Standard of Proof"

In a recent judgment, the ILOAT refused to be drawn on exactly what its standard of proof actually means: "[i]t is undesirable to seek to explain or elaborate upon what, in general, might constitute proof beyond reasonable doubt."[25] The Tribunal was more forthcoming as to what it is not: "[i]t is legally irrelevant, for the purposes of the Tribunal's judicial determination of the complaint, that . . . the same formulation is used in the English common law to establish the standard of proof in criminal proceedings."[26]

The ILOAT has also argued that the imposition of the standard beyond reasonable doubt

> does not exist to create an insuperable barrier for organisations to successfully prosecute disciplinary proceedings against staff members . . . The likelihood of misconduct having occurred is insufficient and does not afford appropriate protection to international civil servants . . . The standard of beyond reasonable doubt derived from the Tribunal's case law as it has evolved over the decades, serves a purpose peculiar to the law of the international civil service.[27]

While the ILOAT thus denies any comparison between its purpose-designed standard of proof and the common law standard for criminal prosecution, if it is to mean anything the standard of beyond reasonable doubt must be a higher standard than the simple preponderance of probabilities, or the requirement of "clear and convincing evidence" which has been adopted by a number of international administrative tribunals in the area of serious misconduct, or the requirement of a set of "precise and concurring presumptions," which was the Tribunal's own standard before *In re Navarro*.[28] In assessing guilt or innocence, there are only so many gradations of conviction that the human mind can embrace, and it seems clear that logically "beyond reasonable doubt" requires something approaching certainty as to the occurrence of the fact alleged, whether this standard of proof is being applied at the Old Bailey or in Geneva.

In the common law jurisdictions, the requirement of proof beyond reasonable doubt is just one element of the system of criminal law, which has its own material rules, such as the law of evidence, and procedures, and includes extensive, even on occasion quite intrusive, powers for the investigating authority, with a correspondingly strict legal framework imposed on the competent judicial authority. It is not

---

[25] *H. (no. 24) v. EPO*, Judgment No. 4047, consideration 10.

[26] Ibid., consideration 6.

[27] *S. (No. 2) v. ICC*, Judgment No. 4362, consideration 8.

[28] See sect. 2.1 above.

obvious that it is appropriate to select a discrete element of this system, developed for particular reasons in a particular context, and apply it in quite a different context for quite different reasons and with different effects.

3.3 The Importance (or Not) of Stating the Standard of Proof

It is not always easy to predict how the ILOAT will handle the indication, or failure to indicate, by the relevant body or authority that they have applied the standard of beyond reasonable doubt. In *G. v. EPO*, for example, it held that "even though the Disciplinary Committee did not expressly use the term 'beyond a reasonable doubt' ... the complainant's misconduct was in fact proven to that standard."[29] The appeal against dismissal was rejected.

Similarly, in *N. L. v. ICC*, the Tribunal noted the manifest "unwillingness" of the investigating unit and the Disciplinary Advisory Board "to treat evidence as proving the alleged misconduct beyond a reasonable doubt ... However, it does not follow that the contrary view is inherently or necessarily wrong."[30] The Tribunal upheld the dismissal decision of the Registrar finding that the misconduct charge had been proven beyond a reasonable doubt.

In *S. (No. 6) v. WIPO*, the Tribunal noted that "Staff Rule 10.1.2(d) of WIPO provides that the applicable standard of proof in disciplinary proceedings is 'clear and convincing evidence'." This did not prevent the Tribunal from applying its own standard of proof and holding that the reference by the Director-General to WIPO's standard "does not detract from the fact that, in substance, the standard of beyond reasonable doubt was met."[31]

In *L. v. WHO*, on the other hand, the Office of Internal Oversight had found "sufficient evidence to support [the finding] that the complainant ... had created an intimidating and hostile work environment." The Director-General took the view that the Office's findings and conclusions "are substantiated beyond a reasonable doubt." Here the Tribunal held that "there is an obvious tension, if not inconsistency, between endorsing a conclusion based on findings of fact about misconduct on the basis of sufficient evidence and a declaration that the misconduct was proved beyond reasonable doubt," and set aside the Director-General's decision.[32]

[29] Judgment No. 4364, consideration 10.
[30] Judgment No. 3862, consideration 23.
[31] Judgment No. 4478, consideration 10.
[32] Judgment No. 4598, consideration 13.

4 "Reasonable Doubt" in Contemporary ILOAT Practice

4.1 *L.-B. v. EPO*: Home Alone?

The judgment in *L.-B. v. EPO* provides a recent example of the ILOAT's application of its standard of proof in practice,[33] which is even more striking as the same set of underlying facts almost certainly[34] gave rise to proceedings before another international administrative tribunal, with a diametrically different result. L.-B.'s ex-husband X was claiming dependent child benefits from ESA at the same time as L.-B. was receiving similar benefits from the EPO; X was dismissed without notice and the sums unduly paid were recovered. While his challenge failed, the report of these other proceedings provides some factual background that does not appear in the report of the ILOAT judgment.[35]

L.-B. married X in 2007, when they were both working for the European Space Agency ("ESA") in Darmstadt, Germany. They divorced the following year. In 2010, L.-B. gave birth to a child, whom X acknowledged as being his issue before the competent local authority; the official documents record that they had joint custody of the child, and that they resided at the same location. In 2011, they both moved to The Netherlands, where they shared rented accommodation; X continued to work for ESA at its Noordwijk site, while L.-B. took up employment at the Rijswijk branch of the European Patent Office ("EPO"). In February 2014, L.-B. gave birth to twins, whom X also acknowledged to be his issue, and who were at the relevant time under their joint custody. The same year, they purchased adjoining terrace houses in Wassenaar, The Netherlands, which were connected at the ground floor and first floor.

By declaring to the EPO, as she did on multiple occasions, that she was "a single parent . . . de facto bringing up a child alone," L.-B. was granted certain social and financial advantages in respect of parental leave which were more favourable than those available to a parent not bringing up their child alone. Seised of her case as a result of an enquiry from ESA, the EPO's Investigative Unit found that L.-B. had misrepresented her true status, which was that of a parent bringing up her children together with their father; her misconduct was qualified as misrepresentation and fraud. The Disciplinary Committee considered unanimously that she and X had planned and created a "non-standard" family situation by having three children, even though divorced, and by moving from their common residence in Germany to a common residence in The Netherlands: first on different floors of the same house,

---

[33] Judgment No. 4491.

[34] While the identities of those concerned have been anonymised, there is clear and convincing evidence that L.-B's ex-husband, appropriately designated "X," was the ESA staff member referred to in the ILOAT judgment; the present chapter presumes this to be so.

[35] ESA Appeals Board, Cases Nos. 108 and 109, 24 October 2017. It is not clear how much of this information was included in the ILOAT case file and hence available to the Tribunal; what is important for our purposes is the ILOAT's reasoning regarding the application of its standard of proof.

and subsequently by buying and joining up adjacent halves of the same building. Although aware of her obligation fully to disclose her situation, L.-B. had failed to do so on several occasions. A majority of the Disciplinary Committee found that she had failed to disclose all facts which could be relevant for the allocation of her benefits, and recommended downgrading; the minority found that she had shown a "repeated lack of honesty" and recommended her dismissal. The President of the EPO decided in favour of dismissal, which she challenged before the ILOAT.

It is in relation to the fact of whether L.-B. was in fact "continuously residing together" with her ex-husband, as the President of the EPO had asserted in the contested decision, that the requirement of proof beyond reasonable doubt kicked in. The Tribunal noted from the report of the Investigation Report the written statement by L.-B. that

> the reason why she kept cohabiting with her ex-husband is because she is a catholic and she wanted her children to '*know their father and have access to him*'(emphasis in original).[36]

The Tribunal noted that "[t]he clear import of this paragraph is that the complainant admitted to having cohabited with her ex-husband and this constituted the explanation why." The fact, however, that this statement appeared in a section of L.-B.'s written response headed "No Co-habitation" was sufficient for the Tribunal to conclude that "[n]ot only was no admission to that effect made by the complainant, [but] the entire hypothesis of co-habitation was being challenged by her."[37] The Tribunal held that in so doing L.-B. had provided a "credible explanation of her circumstances."[38]

In the Tribunal's view, the Disciplinary Committee had not come to a finding of fact that the couple had been cohabiting, but had established instead that L.-B.'s house had two access points to X's adjacent house. For his part, the President of the EPO "must have been satisfied [that] what [L.-B.] was saying was a lie and that by reference to other unspecified evidence he was satisfied, at least inferentially, beyond reasonable doubt the two individually were residing together." The Tribunal found it "difficult to see how this conclusion can be justified, let alone at the standard of beyond reasonable doubt," going on to point out that L.-B. had not admitted to any such common residence as the President claimed, and had alleged that X was babysitting his children "from time to time."[39]

The Tribunal found that "there has been a clear reluctance, or indeed refusal, to accept what L.-B. said was true. Obviously, a person who is guilty of fraud may well often lie and contrive false facts to avoid the consequences of their fraudulent conduct." In the present case, it considered that the fraud thesis "involved an unfair

[36] Consideration 6.

[37] The Tribunal apparently discarded as irrelevant the fact that "as soon as the matter was raised [L.-B.] withdrew her request for parental leave at [the] single parent rate," and offered to repay the monies unduly paid her (Judgment, para 2, p. 2).

[38] Consideration 13.

[39] Consideration 13.

and distorted analysis of the facts ... [so that] a finding of guilt beyond reasonable doubt of the charge alleged could not properly have been made."[40] The evidence "overwhelmingly" supported the conclusion that her declaration that she was a single parent was bona fide and was reasonably based, and L.-B. was therefore entitled to parental leave as a single parent. The dismissal decision was annulled and L.-B. was awarded EUR 30000 damages and EUR 8000 costs.[41]

4.2 Single Parenthood and the Benefits of a "Mistaken" Declaration

The starting point for the Tribunal's legal analysis is the definition of "single parent" set out in Rule 2(a) of the Circular implementing what was then Article 45a[42] of the EPO Service Regulations on entitlement to parental leave. This provides:

> [f]or the purposes of Article 45a of the Service Regulations, a single parent is defined as a permanent employee who declares himself to be de facto bringing up a child alone.

The Tribunal took the view that:

> [i]t is the operative fact of making the declaration that attracts the defined status. No doubt the declaration must be bona fide and be reasonably based. But if it is, the definition is satisfied. The definition operates on the opinion of the employee embodied in the declaration. And the definition, framed in this way, must accommodate the possibility that even if the declaration was bona fide and reasonably based, the employee was mistaken at least as perceived by others.[43]

4.3 A Brief Comment on *L.-B. v. EPO*

The conclusion that the staff member's declaration may be mistaken as long as it is "bona fide and be reasonably based" is a somewhat surprising gloss. It would follow that, to prove that an employee has fraudulently claimed to be a single parent, the Administration would have to demonstrate beyond reasonable doubt that the claimant was not acting in good faith, or that the claim was "not reasonably based," notwithstanding the obvious fact that it is the staff member who is best placed to know what their family situation is.

An alternative interpretation of this provision would start from the premise that the reference to a declaration by the claimant is merely the procedural means of

[40] Consideration 20.

[41] The damages awarded were more than eight times the amount of the monies paid to L.-B. on the basis of her "mistaken" declaration as to her family situation.

[42] At the time of writing, Article 44a EPO Service Regulations.

[43] Consideration 4.

establishing single parenthood, rather than requiring certification of this fact by a third party or public agency, or even by the organisation itself. The provision relied for its application essentially on honesty and a modicum of intelligence on the part of the staff member concerned. L.-B. was claiming a benefit; the sole obligation she had to fulfil to receive it was to make an accurate declaration showing her family situation was such that she was entitled to it. Here the burden of proof falls on L.-B. to demonstrate she fulfils the conditions for entitlement, not on the organisation to prove beyond reasonable doubt that she does not.

A staff member of the EPO is required in all cases to act with integrity and "conduct himself . . . in a manner befitting his status as an international civil servant, embracing honesty, truthfulness, impartiality and incorruptibility";[44] it is thus the staff member who stands guarantor of the veracity of his claim, and should in principle take the consequences of any purported "mistake."[45] This does not appear to be an excessively onerous requirement for the employee. The test is a factual one, and does not require the application of difficult legal concepts; employees surely can be expected to understand whether they are "de facto bringing up a child alone or not." As the Tribunal held in a different context, where a staff member had been found to have falsely claimed social benefits, "[t]here can be no reasonable doubt as to the level of [the complainant's] awareness when it comes to such fundamental facts of [his] life as [his] marriage and divorce, neither as to the aim of benefitting unduly from the [Organization]."[46]

Under this alternative reading, the "operative fact" justifying the status of "single parent" would be a truthful declaration, rather than the mere, possibly erroneous and almost inevitably self-serving, opinion of the claimant. The ILOAT acknowledged L.-B.'s domestic arrangements to be most unusual.[47] In case of doubt, the employee "embracing honesty, truthfulness, impartiality ... incorruptibility" and integrity, such as is demanded of EPO staff, would be expected to disclose the full gamut of facts regarding their situation, to enable the Administration to assess their entitlement, or not, to the status of single parenthood, rather than relying on an idiosyncratic interpretation of the rules. Indeed, the Disciplinary Committee was unanimous in finding L.-B. guilty of misconduct for failing to disclose all the relevant facts about her situation, which a minority considered to be "a repeated lack of honesty." The President of the EPO based his decision to dismiss L.-B. on her breaches of Articles 5(1) and 14(1) of the Service Regulations, rather than on the breach of Rule 2(a) of the Circular on parental leave per se.

---

[44] Articles 5(1) and 14(1), EPO Service Regulations.

[45] Following her interview with the Investigative Unit, L.-B. withdrew her request for parental leave at the single-parent rate, thereby implicitly acknowledging that her previous declarations were mistaken, and that she was not in fact entitled to the single-parent rate.

[46] *G. v. EPO* Judgment No. 4364, consideration 10.

[47] Consideration 9, p. 8.

4.4 How to Dispel "Reasonable Doubt"

In the present case, in order properly to demonstrate beyond reasonable doubt that L.-B. was not in fact bringing up her children "alone," the Investigative Unit of the EPO would in principle have needed powers comparable to those enjoyed by a police force. This would have included the possibility to inspect *in situ* (presumably under cover of a warrant) the disposition of the building in which L.-B. and X indisputably resided, to assess the respective presence of children's clothing, toys, and other accoutrements in each part of the residence(s), examine the state of the financial, social and personal relations between L.-B. and X, their holiday and leisure arrangements, the extent of X's babysitting activities (if any) for his own children, and so on. The Investigative Unit would also have needed to have been able to seize the parents' mobile phones to assess the range and nature of X's contribution to the bringing up of the children (if any) as demonstrated in any relevant calls, texts, messages, photos and videos; to gain access to their email and social media accounts for the same purpose; question witnesses, such as neighbours in Wassenaar who would be familiar with the comings and goings of L.-B. and X, staff at any shops frequented by either or both parents, staff at any nursery school or other childcare facility used by L.-B.'s children, and colleagues and family of both parents, and, of course, and very significantly, interview X under threat of perjury. In this context, the Administration of the EPO would have been able to take account of the fact that, during the years L.-B. was claiming to be bringing up her child (later, children) "alone," X had declared to ESA that the children "depend[ed] on him or his household for [their] main and continuing support."[48]

It is not suggested that any international organisation should enjoy such exorbitant powers with regard to its own staff, still less with respect to private individuals and entities outside the organisation in the context of investigations of misconduct by its staff. However, the imposition of a standard of proof which is, in practical if not in legal terms, the equivalent of that applied in the criminal law of the common law jurisdictions without the necessary powers to satisfy it risks requiring the organisation to prove matters which it is materially incapable of doing.

4.5 Paternal Parenting

On a different point of fact, the Tribunal also held that "[t]here is a significant difference, at least potentially, between 'living with' and 'bringing up'" children.[49] As a matter of semantics, this may be true; its soundness in the circumstance of the

[48] ESA Appeals Board, Cases No. 108 and 109, para 63(i); this judgment was handed down on 24 October 2017, six months before L.-B. filed her appeal with the ILOAT and more than four years before the *L.-B.* judgment. As noted above, the investigation of L.-B.'s conduct was initiated following a query from the ESA administration.

[49] Consideration 12.

present case is more open to doubt. For two of the three years in which L.-B. was taking parental leave putatively as a "single parent ... de facto bringing up a child alone," her household included three children of six years or younger, including twins under two years old. One struggles to imagine how X, being their father, could have "lived with" his young child, later children, and not have contributed to their "bringing up" at this time or indeed, if this were the case, why L.-B. would have allowed him into her area of the shared building in the first place, if he were not contributing to the "bringing up" of his own child(ren).

5 Standard of Proof in Harassment Disputes

5.1 Proving Harassment Allegations: "The Further Off from England, the Nearer Is to France"

The most controversial application of the ILOAT's standard of proof beyond reasonable doubt is in the area of claims of harassment by one staff member against another. Unlike most incidents which may ultimately give rise to disciplinary proceedings, in this context, and contrary to what the ILOAT appears to believe,[50] there are in fact three parties whose interests are at stake: the alleged victim, the alleged harasser, and the organisation. While the harassment of a staff member can have gravely deleterious effects on the health, and particularly the mental health, and wellbeing of the victim, an allegation of harassing behaviour may potentially constitute a serious blight on the career and the wellbeing of the alleged harasser. For this reason, the staff rules of some organisations provide that a false accusation of harassment, or one which is made in bad faith, is in itself a disciplinary offence; the ILOAT is careful to specify that only the alleged victim who acts in good faith is protected from repercussions on account of their allegations.[51] Meanwhile, the organisation has obligations with regard to each of the protagonists: as the ILOAT held, for example, in *E. v. FAO*, "an accusation of harassment requires that an international organization both investigate the matter thoroughly and accord full due process and protection to the person accused."[52]

It follows from the character of a harassment complaint that, as a matter of principle, the higher the standard of proof for the organisation to make a finding of harassing behaviour, the more difficult it is for the victim to have their complaint recognised as valid. The two standards of proof may be likened to communicating vessels.

The difficulty of proving harassment is exacerbated by the fact that, where there are only two protagonists, a single alleged victim and a single alleged harasser, there are rarely any witnesses to the incidents complained of, and usually no paper trail.

[50] See discussion of Judgment No. 4207, *G.M. v. IAEA*, sect. 7.2 below.

[51] Loc. cit.

[52] Judgment No. 3593, consideration 12 (internal punctuation omitted).

This is particularly true with respect to allegations of sexual harassment. Thus in *P. v. UNESCO*, for example, the putative harasser was alleged to have kissed the victim on the mouth against her will when no witness was present; before the Tribunal he contended that the opening of the investigation was illegal because "the allegations of the sole complainant ... were unsupported by any material evidence." The ILOAT acknowledged that "the nature of the act in question ... made it impossible to produce any evidence of this kind."[53] In that case, the harassment complaint was only rendered credible, and was eventually upheld, thanks to plentiful evidence of similar behaviour on the part of the alleged harasser against other women. It is difficult to see how the organisation could have found the alleged harasser guilty of such behaviour beyond reasonable doubt in this case were it not for the fortuitous existence of such other evidence, and the exceptional courage of the harasser's other victims. A sexual predator who is careful to act when in the sole company of her or, more probably, his chosen victim would by this token be able to act with impunity.

5.2 The Standard of Proof in Disciplinary Proceedings Against an Alleged Harasser

The case of *H. (No. 24) v. EPO* illustrates the operation of this standard of proof in practice in relation to psychological harassment.[54] H. was found guilty by the EPO's Disciplinary Committee of the unauthorised disclosure of internal, confidential and personal material, threatening and harassing other members of staff, and inappropriate behaviour during the investigation of alleged offences and the conduct of disciplinary procedures. The Committee took the view that H.'s behaviour was likely to continue and concluded that the appropriate sanction was dismissal. The President agreed and dismissed her. In her appeal to the ILOAT, H. contended in particular that the President had not applied the standard of proof beyond reasonable doubt.

The Tribunal found that H. had not admitted any of the charges and that both the Disciplinary Committee and the President were therefore required to establish guilt beyond reasonable doubt: "[t]here would be no utility in the Disciplinary Committee applying some other standard before reporting to the President."[55] While the Committee had found that " there exist[ed] independent evidence to substantiate each and every one of the allegations against [H.]," the Tribunal held that this test "allows for the possibility that there was other evidence pointing in the other direction."[56] The Tribunal further considered that "in this case, were there such other evidence, it

[53] Judgment No. 3640, consideration 5.

[54] Judgment 4047, 26 June 2018

[55] Consideration 9.

[56] Consideration 10.

probably would be difficult to be satisfied to that standard of proof."[57] In respect to two of the charges, the President had either failed to refer to the standard of proof or applied a " substantial evidence" rule; though he had expressed his lack of doubt with respect to one instance of conduct in the other charge, he had not done so regarding the repetition of such conduct. On this occasion, the President's decision was annulled and the matter was remitted to the EPO to be "considered afresh by a differently constituted Disciplinary Committee and for the President of the Office to make a new decision." In the meantime, the Tribunal awarded H. EUR 20000 in moral damages and EUR 7000 in costs.

Whatever the possible merits of the Tribunal's ruling in this case, it gives rise to a number of practical issues. Particularly, although H. was found guilty by a unanimous Disciplinary Committee of threatening and harassing EPO staff, with aggravating circumstances and a likelihood of recidivism, the EPO could find itself powerless to take measures to protect the victims of H.'s harassment, insofar as those measures could be construed as implied disciplinary measures against H.

The Tribunal also noted that, before the Disciplinary Committee had adopted its report, H. had made certain statements "which might be thought to constitute express or tacit acceptance of the fact concerning her conduct and her reasons underlying her conduct [which] may constitute admissions against interest which, in an evidentiary sense, are relevant in determining what are the facts."[58] The ILOAT has always accepted that where the facts are "uncontroverted," these can be considered as proven beyond reasonable doubt without more, even in proceedings where the Organisation has failed to specify the correct standard of proof.[59]

In *H. (No. 24) v. EPO*, however, the Tribunal took the view that a statement made by H., after the Committee's report but before the President's decision, which resiled on her previous admissions "imposed an obligation on the EPO to assess the material by applying the test of beyond reasonable doubt."[60] This means that, even where a staff member admits the facts during the disciplinary procedure, the organisation would be required to prove them beyond reasonable doubt to prevent the staff member from sending the procedure back to square one by the simple expedient of withdrawing her previous admissions after the procedure is over. Would such a volte-face after a judgment of the ILOAT upholding a finding of misconduct against a staff member on the basis of "uncontroverted facts" require the Tribunal to "assess the material by applying the test of beyond reasonable doubt" too?

---

[57] Loc. cit. This sentence is not easy to understand in English; from the French version, it appears that the Tribunal may have intended to indicate that the existence of such evidence would mean that the requirement of proof beyond reasonable doubt could not be satisfied.

[58] Consideration 7.

[59] *G. v. EPO,* Judgment No. 4364.

[60] Consideration 10.

6 Reactions to the ILOAT's Case Law

6.1 Other International Organisations: Not in My Name

The ILOAT's singular stance on the standard of proof has been criticised by experts in the field of harassment in the workplace. The panel of independent experts commissioned by UNAIDS to examine the prevention of and response to harassment, bullying and abuse of power at the UNAIDS secretariat did not mince their words on the subject of the standard of proof:

> The data shows that a majority of claims when investigated by IOS are held to be unsubstantiated. One reason for the preponderance of unsubstantiated complaints lies in the erroneous and misplaced high standard of proof employed by IOS, which requires misconduct to be proved beyond a reasonable doubt. This high standard has had a chilling effect on IOS investigating complaints where it finds that the standard cannot be reached in the absence of corroborative or independent evidence of the alleged incident.
>
> [149.] The Panel considers that the high standard of proof has been adopted in error, with the effect of denying a comprehensive investigation of complaints whenever IOS believes that the standard cannot be achieved ...There will be ... cases where, even though an investigation has been carried out, the higher standard of proof may not be achieved. In both these situations the high standard of proof may have led to a failure to protect staff from oppressive misconduct.
>
> [150.] The argument in favour of the higher standard is that consequences of an adverse finding are very serious. However, disciplinary proceedings are not criminal trials where the charge is required to be proved beyond reasonable doubt since the penal consequences include deprivation of personal liberty. In disciplinary proceedings, stringent and technical rules of evidence need not be applied. The Panel believes that to provide sufficient protection to staff, and to protect the laws and values of the UN, the standard of proof should be a test akin to the common law civil standard of proof, i.e. the balance of probabilities or a preponderance of evidence.

After quoting with approval the rejection of this standard of proof by the UNAT, the panel concluded:

> The high standard now in effect fails to take account of the serious consequences for the complainant who is stigmatised and left vulnerable when a complaint is rejected. Indeed, there are also damaging impacts on UNAIDS if an alleged perpetrator of serious misconduct is left free to continue their employment amongst colleagues who perceive they 'have got away with it.'[61]

The following year, advisors to IFAD's Executive Board expressed concern that the ILOAT's standard of proof "does not allow the Fund to react properly in disciplinary cases, including ensuring the full implementation of its zero tolerance towards sexual harassment (SH), sexual exploitation and abuse (SEA),

[61] Report on the work of the Independent Expert Panel on prevention of and response to harassment, including sexual harassment; bullying and abuse of power at UNAIDS Secretariat | UNAIDS.

anticorruption and other crucial disciplinary issues."[62] They identified this as one of the principal reasons for its proposal that IFAD withdraw from the jurisdiction of the ILOAT in favour of that of UNAT. Their note to the Executive Board observes that a significant number of other entities subject to ILOAT's jurisdiction have also expressed similar concerns regarding the standard of proof it applies and that "within the last couple of years, various agencies have opted to leave the ILOAT."[63]

6.2 The International Labour Organization

The ILOAT's host organisation, the International Labour Organization, proposed amendments to the ILOAT Statute which tightened the conditions under which an organisation may withdraw from ILOAT jurisdiction.[64] Clause 3 of the Annex to the Statute now requires a withdrawing organisation to act "in keeping with the principles of good faith and transparency" and to reaffirm its commitment "to faithfully execute judgments on any pending cases and indicat[e] ... the reasons for withdrawing its recognition of the Tribunal's jurisdiction."

7 *Eppur si muove*: A Shift in the ILOAT Case Law?

7.1 G.M. v. IAEA

Whether or not by way of reaction to criticism from some of its client entities and peer tribunals, the ILOAT has nuanced its position on the standard of proof in harassment cases in recent times.

By way of a prelude, in *R. v. UNIDO*, the ILOAT held that the task of the Organisation's investigation unit, the Internal Oversight Service ("IOS"), was to "determine whether there is sufficient information to substantiate a complaint on the balance of probabilities." The complainant, against whom a variety of serious disciplinary charges had been upheld, argued that the Joint Disciplinary Committee could not come to a finding beyond reasonable doubt on the basis of a report which had applied a lower standard of proof.[65] The Tribunal held, however, that the Committee had not relied solely on the report of the IOS, as it also had before it "among other things, the written statement provided by the complainant"; while the Committee had expressed "reservations concerning aspects of the IOS's investigation and Report, [these] did not detract from the [Committee]'s conclusions and

[62] *IFAD's Appeal Process: Assessment and Recommendations*, 6 May 2019, EB-2019-126-R-35.pdf (ifad.org).

[63] IFAD renounced ILOAT's jurisdiction with effect from 31 March 2020; in total, ten organisations have done so, eight of them since 2016.

[64] *IFAD's Appeal Process*, para 12, p. 3.

[65] Judgment No. 3725, consideration 14; the Guidelines are quoted verbatim at consideration 10.

recommendations." The Tribunal noted that the Committee had found "sufficient evidence" to support two of the charges against the complainant and held that it "could have reasonably come to these conclusions on the totality of the evidence beyond a reasonable doubt."[66]

The Tribunal set out its thinking in this area in *G.M. v. IAEA* (2020), where the administration's handling of a complaint of sexual harassment was decisively influenced, one might even say hampered, by the ILOAT's then case law on the standard of proof in disciplinary matters.[67] G.M. was a female staff member of more than 14 years' standing at IAEA when Mr. A was appointed to the same section at a higher grade. Within a month, she had complained to her Head of Section that she had been subjected to sexual harassment by A, a complaint she repeated on subsequent occasions, given A's "persisting pattern of unwelcome behaviour." G.M. was advised to "take assertiv[ness] training . . . and . . . to be less friendly."[68] Her complaint was eventually forwarded for investigation to the Office of Internal Oversight Services ("OIOS"), which reported as follows:

> [a]s it is often the case in sexual harassment complaints, there are no independent witnesses. As such, evidence must be adduced which tends to show the respective credibility of the principals.[69]

The OIOS acknowledged that G.M.'s reporting of the incidents was consistent, that she had reported these to colleagues, and that her complaint was "credible and made in good faith." On the other hand, in the light of A's "vehement denials," his apology to G.M., and the absence of any witnesses, the OIOS found that "there was inadequate evidence upon which it could properly be concluded that . . . harassment was established beyond a reasonable doubt." In fine, the OIOS reported that it could "not make a conclusive determination in this case."

Although informed that the investigation was closed, G.M. had to wait another 15 months to be apprised of the outcome of her complaint. The Director for Human Resources informed her that A. was to be issued a letter of warning, reminded of his managerial responsibilities, advised to respect the staff rules, and directed to undergo training on the IAEA's policies on sexual harassment. On the other hand, the Director concluded that there was inadequate evidence to establish harassment beyond a reasonable doubt. In answer to G.M.'s request for review, the Director-General decided that "no breach of [her] rights [had been] identified and [her] request . . . for compensation for alleged material or moral damages in connection with the reported harassment was denied." G.M. challenged this decision before the

[66] Considerations 18 and 19. There is no indication in the case report that the Committee did, in fact, come to its conclusions "beyond a reasonable doubt," but this does not appear to have troubled the Tribunal.

[67] Judgment No. 4207; the case was, exceptionally, heard en banc.

[68] Consideration 1; rape victims everywhere, take note!

[69] Final Investigation Report, para 56, quoted at consideration 3.

Tribunal, where the IAEA argued, inter alia, that the Director-General had been obliged to apply the standard of proof beyond reasonable doubt.

The Tribunal noted that the IAEA staff rules provided for both an investigation process ("Appendix E" to the Administrative Manual) and a disciplinary process ("Appendix G") to deal with reported misconduct: "the purpose of Appendix G is to determine whether the subject staff member is guilty of the reported misconduct ... which may result in the imposition of a disciplinary measure." The pivotal finding of the Tribunal merits being quoted *in extenso*:

> [a] claim of harassment and a report of misconduct based on an allegation of harassment are distinct and separate matters. A claim of harassment is a claim addressed to the organization the resolution of which only involves two parties, the organization and the reporter of the harassment. In contrast, a report of alleged misconduct, based on an allegation of harassment, triggers the Appendix G procedures, a process that is directed at the culpability of the staff member in question and potentially the imposition of a disciplinary measure. In this process, the two parties are the organization and the staff member in question. In this process, the report of the misconduct, a potential victim of the harassment, is a witness and not a party to the proceedings.[70]

The Tribunal concluded that the IEAE had applied an incorrect standard of proof to G.M.'s complaint: "the applicable standard of proof for a finding of harassment in a case such as this is not 'beyond a reasonable doubt' but a less onerous standard." As there was "sufficient evidence and information in the pleadings for the Tribunal to make an informed decision," the ILOAT went on itself to consider the merits of G. M.'s complaint of sexual harassment, and held that this was substantiated. It awarded G.M. EUR 25000 for the harassment, the "inexplicable, unreasonable delay and the significant harm she suffered due to this delay."[71]

Logically it follows from *G.M. v. IAEA* that a body charged with handling a complaint for harassment may not apply the standard of proof beyond reasonable doubt in coming to its conclusions. This the ILOAT confirmed in *S. v. ICGEB*, where it held that this higher standard "has no application in the assessment of the claim of harassment where the staff member is seeking workplace protection or damages or both."[72]

7.2 Potential Repercussions of *G.M. v. IAEA*

The ILOAT's ruling in *G.M. v. IAEA* implies that an international organisation must necessarily have two distinct procedures for dealing with harassment allegations,

[70] Consideration 14.

[71] Judgment, considerations 20–22. The amount is only slightly more than that awarded to H., the disciplinary charges against whom were sufficiently plausible to be remitted to the organisation, and slightly less than granted L.-B., who was unable to determine whether she was "alone" in bringing up her three small children under the same roof as their father.

[72] Judgment No. 4289, consideration 10.

one for a claim for protection against such (alleged) behaviour, another for dealing with the disciplinary investigation and punishment of harassment which has been found. Where "there are no specific provisions in [the organization's staff rules] that articulate a comprehensive procedure to deal with a claim [for protection against] harassment," the organisation is still under a duty to "provide a safe and adequate working environment for its staff members" and "given the serious nature of a claim of harassment . . . has an obligation to initiate the investigation itself."[73]

That an international organisation must provide a harassment-free work environment and take the necessary initiatives to this end is unexceptionable, but it does not necessarily follow that requiring two separate procedures to deal with what are essentially the same facts is the most appropriate means to achieve this objective. The IAEA is not the only international organisation which takes the view that harassment complaints and investigation of misconduct for harassment are not necessarily "distinct and separate matters," and therefore charges the organ responsible for disciplinary matters to investigate formal complaints of harassment against a staff member.[74]

If a harassment claim has been made and parallel "protection" and "misconduct" procedures conducted, the organisation could end up adopting contradictory decisions on the basis of the same facts, where the claim for protection is upheld, but the misconduct charge is rejected owing to the difficulty of reaching the higher standard of proof. In this scenario, measures taken by the organisation against the harasser run the risk of being challenged as disguised disciplinary sanctions. As Szabo has observed, "[b]y creating two standards in respect of the same conduct, the [ILOAT] judgments will make it more difficult for organizations to manage a harassment-free working environment . . . [where] organizations may become liable to victims of workplace harassment for injury caused to them, while perpetrators remain unaccountable for their actions".[75]

The ILOAT's approach, moreover, could have the effect of undermining the value of the work of the body investigating the allegations of harassment. The Tribunal has long recognised that the investigative body "as the primary trier of fact, has had the benefit of actually seeing and hearing many of the persons involved, and of assessing the reliability of what they have said. For that reason such a body is entitled to considerable deference," and the Tribunal "will only interfere in the case of manifest error."[76] As such a body operates under the balance of probabilities,[77] the Disciplinary Committee will be unable in principle to rely on its findings alone in

[73] Judgment 4207, consideration 15.

[74] For the ICC, for example, see ICC Administrative Instructions ICC/AI/2005/005 and ICC/AI/2008/001.

[75] Szabo (in press), this volume.

[76] *E. v. FAO*, Judgment No. 3953, consideration 12.

[77] *R. v. UNIDO*, footnote 61 above, consideration 14.

reaching its own conclusions beyond reasonable doubt, as the Tribunal acknowledged implicitly in *R. v. UNIDO*.

It is, moreover, considered in many quarters that, where protection is not an immediate issue, what staff members who complain of harassment want most is neither compensation nor revenge but vindication, the formal recognition that their personal dignity has been undermined by the acts of another person. In this regard, the European Union's now defunct specialist civil service court held that "a finding by the administration that psychological harassment has occurred is, in itself, likely to have a beneficial effect in the therapeutic process of recovery of an individual who has been harassed."[78] Thus, while in theory the benefit of the finding of harassment is not affected by the rejection of a misconduct charge against the harasser, complainants are in fact likely to consider that the recognition of the acts of which they were victims has been undermined if not negated, while future victims of harassment may thereby be discouraged from even making a complaint, if they understand the harasser is unlikely to be subject to any sanction.[79]

There may also be situations where a separate proceeding for protection against harassment is redundant, for example, if the alleged victim or alleged harasser has left the organisation, or where for any other reason the alleged victim does not wish any such proceeding to be carried out, or where the investigation of alleged harassment has been launched at the initiative of the organisation, for example at the behest of the staff association, as in *P. v. PAHO*.[80] In these circumstances, the organisation would in principle only be left with the option of commencing a disciplinary procedure, using the standard of proof beyond reasonable doubt. Should the organisation fail to reach what is undeniably a high bar—which may be particularly difficult precisely because there is no alleged victim present and only third party witnesses—then the harasser would be free to harass other members of staff, or at least escape any disciplinary sanction.

Arguably, it is not the absence of a separate "protection from harassment" procedure which fails to secure a "safe and adequate working environment for ... staff members" in international institutions, but the imposition of an inappropriate and unrealistic standard of proof to establish that harassment has occurred.

8 Concluding Remarks

Apart from a number of practical conundra above, the ILOAT's application of a standard of proof beyond reasonable doubt in the area of harassment disputes generally poses two questions of wider scope.

[78] Case F-95/09 *Skareby v. Commission* EU:F:2011:9, para 26, and adopted by the Court of Justice (Case C-187/19 P, *EEAS v. De Loecker*, EU:C:2020:444, para 74).

[79] The alleged victim of harassment in *L. (No. 2) v. ICC* accepted in effect that her complaint would need to be "prove[n] beyond reasonable doubt": Judgment No. 4475, p. 3.

[80] Judgment No. 4674, p. 1.

The first concerns the institutional autonomy of the organisations to determine both the procedures they apply to deal with workplace harassment and the standard of proof they choose to apply. The Tribunal has acknowledged that it must apply the different definitions of "harassment" adopted by each organisation under its supervision, "since the definitions form part of the applicable law for each organization against which a case is filed."[81] It is, therefore, all the more surprising that the Tribunal has in effect imposed its own view of the appropriate standard of proof in disciplinary cases, and the proper internal procedures for ensuring staff are protected against harassment, as if these were not "part of the applicable law for each organization." Ironically, when it first adopted this standard in *In re Navarro*, the ILOAT was prima facie respecting the standard of proof on which the respondent organisation was apparently relying.

Second, it is difficult to avoid the conclusion that the net result of the ILOAT's case law on the standard of proof is that a proportion, perhaps even a significant proportion, of wrongdoers can act with impunity, where the services of the organisation do not enjoy sufficiently strong investigative powers to be able to garner proof beyond reasonable doubt. Such a situation was surely not intended by those who established the international civil service and granted it immunity from the jurisdiction of the local authorities of their place of establishment.

This state of affairs may be considered particularly regrettable with respect to those who have been victims of acts of psychological or sexual harassment at the workplace. Perhaps the Tribunal should pause to consider the lofty ambitions of its mother organisation, the International Labour Organization, whose Convention on Violence and Harassment recognises

> the right of everyone to a world of work free from . . . harassment, including gender-based . . . harassment,

reminds Members of their

> important responsibility to promote a general environment of zero tolerance to . . . harassment in order to facilitate the prevention of such behaviors and practices,

and calls on

> all actors in the world of work [to] refrain from, prevent and address . . . harassment.[82]

* * *

[81] Petrovic (2021), p. 185.

[82] ILO Violence and Harassment Convention No. 190 of 21 June 2019; entry into force 25 June 2021.

References

Peay, M. (in press). Divergent standards of proof currently applied by International Administrative Tribunals in Serious Misconduct Cases: An evolving snapshot. In Bravo T, Bradley K (eds) (this volume).

Petrovic, D. (2021) Acts of international conference organised by the Court of Justice of the Eurasian Economic Union on 25–27 November 2020, Minsk: 183–195.

Szabo, R. (in press). Harassment Investigations in International Organizations: Rights of claimants under the jurisprudence of the International Labour Organization Administrative Tribunal. In Bravo T, Bradley K (eds) (this volume).

Tavadian, A., & Ducamin, C. (2023). Proliferation of standards of proof in International Administrative Tribunals. *The Law and Practice of International Courts and Tribunals, 22*, 137–160.

MIX
Papier aus verantwortungsvollen Quellen
Paper from responsible sources
FSC® C105338

If you have any concerns about our products,
you can contact us on
ProductSafety@springernature.com

In case Publisher is established outside the EU,
the EU authorized representative is:
Springer Nature Customer Service Center GmbH
Europaplatz 3, 69115 Heidelberg, Germany

Printed by Libri Plureos GmbH
in Hamburg, Germany